The Classic Civil Aircraft Guide

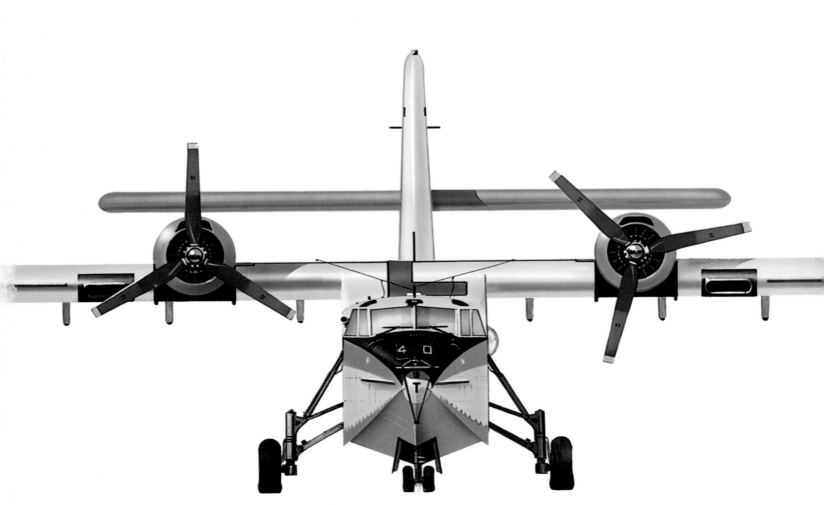

The Classic Civil Aircraft Guide

Editor: David Donald

CHARTWELL
BOOKS, INC.

Published by
CHARTWELL BOOKS, INC.
A Division of **BOOK SALES, INC.**
114 Northfield Avenue
Edison, New Jersey 08837

Copyright © 1999 Orbis Publishing Ltd
Copyright © 1999 Aerospace Publishing Ltd

Some of this material has previously appeared in the
Orbis reference set 'Airplane'.

ISBN: 0-7858-1089-7

Editorial and design by
Brown Packaging Books Ltd
Bradley's Close
74–77 White Lion Street
London N1 9PF

Editor: David Donald

Printed in The Czech Republic

Contents

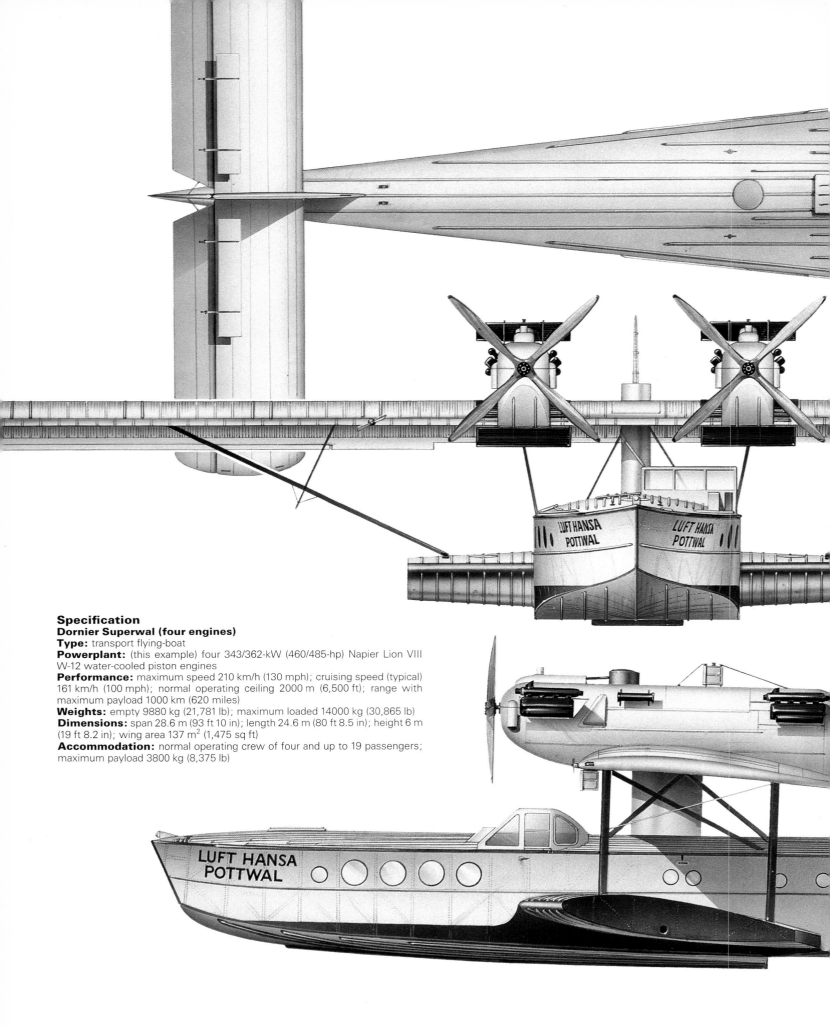

Specification
Dornier Superwal (four engines)
Type: transport flying-boat
Powerplant: (this example) four 343/362-kW (460/485-hp) Napier Lion VIII W-12 water-cooled piston engines
Performance: maximum speed 210 km/h (130 mph); cruising speed (typical) 161 km/h (100 mph); normal operating ceiling 2000 m (6,500 ft); range with maximum payload 1000 km (620 miles)
Weights: empty 9880 kg (21,781 lb); maximum loaded 14000 kg (30,865 lb)
Dimensions: span 28.6 m (93 ft 10 in); length 24.6 m (80 ft 8.5 in); height 6 m (19 ft 8.2 in); wing area 137 m^2 (1,475 sq ft)
Accommodation: normal operating crew of four and up to 19 passengers; maximum payload 3800 kg (8,375 lb)

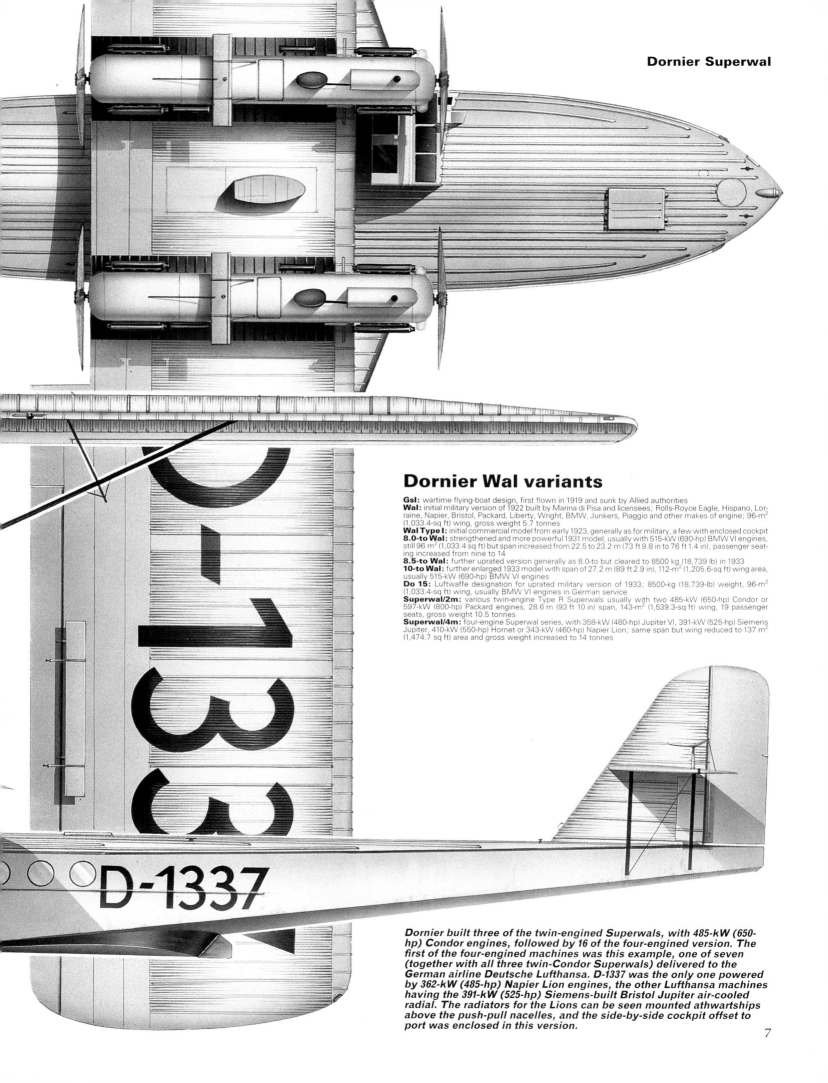

Dornier Superwal

Dornier Wal variants

Gsl: wartime flying-boat design, first flown in 1919 and sunk by Allied authorities
Wal: initial military version of 1922 built by Marina di Pisa and licensees; Rolls-Royce Eagle, Hispano, Lor-raine, Napier, Bristol, Packard, Liberty, Wright, BMW, Junkers, Piaggio and other makes of engine; 96-m² (1,033.4-sq ft) wing, gross weight 5.7 tonnes
Wal Type I: initial commercial model from early 1923, generally as for military, a few with enclosed cockpit
8.0-to Wal: strengthened and more powerful 1931 model, usually with 515-kW (690-hp) BMW VI engines, still 96 m² (1,033.4 sq ft) but span increased from 22.5 to 23.2 m (73 ft 9.8 in to 76 ft 1.4 in); passenger seat-ing increased from nine to 14
8.5-to Wal: further uprated version generally as 8.0-to but cleared to 8500 kg (18,739 lb) in 1933
10-to Wal: further enlarged 1933 model with span of 27.2 m (89 ft 2.9 in), 112-m² (1,205.6-sq ft) wing area, usually 515-kW (690-hp) BMW VI engines
Do 15: Luftwaffe designation for uprated military version of 1933; 8500-kg (18,739-lb) weight, 96-m² (1,033.4-sq ft) wing, usually BMW VI engines in German service
Superwal/2m: various twin-engine Type R Superwals usually with two 485-kW (650-hp) Condor or 597-kW (800-hp) Packard engines, 28.6 m (93 ft 10 in) span, 143-m² (1,539.3-sq ft) wing, 19 passenger seats, gross weight 10.5 tonnes
Superwal/4m: four-engine Superwal series, with 358-kW (480-hp) Jupiter VI, 391-kW (525-hp) Siemens Jupiter, 410-kW (550-hp) Hornet or 343-kW (460-hp) Napier Lion; same span but wing reduced to 137 m² (1,474.7 sq ft) area and gross weight increased to 14 tonnes

Dornier built three of the twin-engined Superwals, with 485-kW (650-hp) Condor engines, followed by 16 of the four-engined version. The first of the four-engined machines was this example, one of seven (together with all three twin-Condor Superwals) delivered to the German airline Deutsche Lufthansa. D-1337 was the only one powered by 362-kW (485-hp) Napier Lion engines, the other Lufthansa machines having the 391-kW (525-hp) Siemens-built Bristol Jupiter air-cooled radial. The radiators for the Lions can be seen mounted athwartships above the push-pull nacelles, and the side-by-side cockpit offset to port was enclosed in this version.

7

D.H.82A Tiger Moth Mk II

Specification
D.H.82A Tiger Moth Mk II
Type: two-seat *ab initio* trainer biplane
Powerplant: one 97-kW (130-hp) de Havilland Gipsy Major I four-cylinder air-cooled inverted inline piston engine
Performance: maximum speed 167 km/h (104 mph) at sea level; initial climb rate 194 m (635 ft) per minute; service ceiling 4145 m (13,600 ft); range 483 km (300 miles)
Weights: empty 506 kg (1,115 lb); maximum take-off 828 kg (1,825 lb)
Dimensions: span 8.94 m (29 ft 4 in); length 7.29 m (23 ft 11 in); height 2.68 m (8 ft 9½ in); wing area 22.20 m² (239 sq ft)
Armament: none

M. Badrocke

A de Havilland D.H.82A Tiger Moth of the University of London Air Squadron based at RAF Fairoaks in 1950. The University Air Squadrons received Tiger Moths to replace Avro Tutors in 1939, retaining them until they received de Havilland Chipmunks in the early 1950s. The RUL code prefix on this aircraft signifies Reserve Command, University of London Air Squadron, and it carries standard post-war yellow training bands on its fuselage and wings. This aircraft is fitted with a blind flying hood for instrument flying training; in use this would unfold on a metal framework to cover the rear cockpit.

Moth variants

D.H.60 Moth (Cirrus I): 1925-26 model; two prototypes (G-EBKT and G-EBKU); eight pre-production; 31 production aircraft

D.H.60 Moth (Cirrus II): 1926-27 model; 32 built

D.H.60 Genet Moth: six aircraft (J8816-J8821) for Air Ministry; Genet engines

D.H.60X Moth (Cirrus III): 1928 model; 338 built by de Havilland at Stag Lane

D.H.60G Gipsy Moth: introduced 1928; 595 built by de Havilland at Stag Lane; 40 aircraft built by Morane-Saulnier in France; 18 built by Moth Aircraft Corp. in USA; 32 built by Larkin Aircraft Supply, Melbourne, for Australian government

D.H.60M Moth (Metal Moth): introduced 1928; four pre-production aircraft; 536 built by de Havilland at Stag Lane; 40 built by DH Canada; 161 built by Moth Aircraft Corp. in USA; 10 built by Norwegian Army Aircraft Factory in 1931

D.H.60G-III Moth: Gipsy III in wooden Moth; introduced in 1932; 47 built by de Havilland at Stag Lane

D.H.60G-III Moth Major: Gipsy Major III or IIIA; introduced in 1934; one prototype (G-ACNP) and 96 production aircraft

D.H.60T Moth Trainer: Gipsy II; military trainer; introduced 1931; two prototypes (G-ABKS and G-ABKU) and initial production of 47 aircraft

D.H.61 Giant Moth: six/eight-passenger cabin biplane; Jupiter VI or XI, Jaguar VIC or Pratt & Whitney Hornet engine; introduced 1928

D.H.71 Tiger Moth: two experimental monoplanes, G-EBQU (Gipsy) and G-EBRV (Cirrus II) produced in 1927

D.H.75 Hawk Moth: first high-wing Moth; one D.H.75 prototype (de Havilland Ghost engine), five **D.H.75A** (Lynx, Whirlwind or Cheetah engine), and one **D.H.75B** (Whirlwind)

D.H.80A Puss Moth: high-wing cabin monoplane; Gipsy III, Gipsy Major or Gipsy (high compression) engine; introduced 1930; one **D.H.80** prototype (G-AAHZ) and 259 production aircraft built by de Havilland at Stag Lane; 25 built by DH Canada

D.H.81 Swallow Moth: two-seat low-wing monoplane, only one built

D.H.82T Tiger Moth: eight aircraft similar to D.H.60T but with Gipsy III; service trials led to D.H.82 and D.H.82A

D.H.82 Tiger Moth: 114 initial military training biplanes built by de Havilland at Stag Lane

D.H.82A Tiger Moth: in RAF, **Tiger Moth Mk II:** basic *ab initio* trainer; total of about 7,290 produced between 1934 and 1945; 795 built by de Havilland at Hatfield, 3,216 by Morris at Cowley, remainder by DH Canada, DH Australia, DH New Zealand, and in Portugal (91), Norway (37) and Sweden (23); Gipsy III and Gipsy Major (various versions); total includes 786 **D.H.82C** with Menasco Pirate D4 engine built by DH Canada (200 sold to USA as **PT-24** in 1942); at least 17 converted to **Thruxton Jackaroo** (four-seat cabin conversion), 1957-59

D.H.82B Queen Bee: radio-controlled gunnery target; RAF 380 Royal Navy 420

D.H.83 Fox Moth: four-passenger cabin biplane; introduced in 1932; Gipsy Major or Gipsy Major IC; total 153

D.H.85A Leopard Moth: three seat high-wing cabin monoplane; introduced in 1933; Gipsy Major (**D.H.85**) and Gipsy Six R (**D.H.85A**); one prototype (G-ACHD) and 131 production aircraft

D.H.87 Hornet Moth: two-seat cabin biplane; introduced in 1934; Gipsy Major I; prototype D.H.87 (G-ACTA), **D.H.87A** with elliptical wings and tips, **D.H.87B** with squared wings and tips; 163 production aircraft

D.H.94 Moth Minor: two-seat low-wing monoplane; introduced in 1937

Junkers F 13da

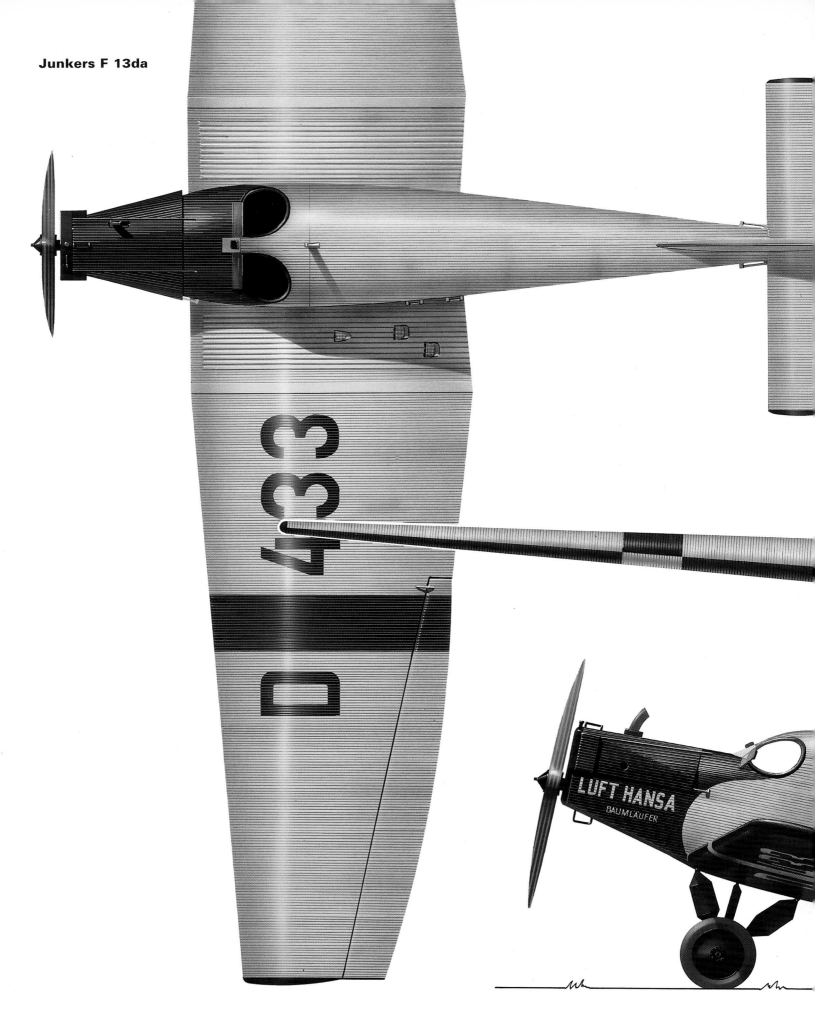

The Junkers F 13 was produced in many versions, mainly with differing engines. The largest user was *Deutsche Lufthansa*, which was formed in 1926 as the German national airline. Most of its aircraft had previously served with *Junkers-Luftverkehr*, an airline started in 1921 by the F 13's manufacturer. F 13s served *DLH* until 1938, when they were transferred to Luftwaffe training schools and pleasure flying companies.

Specification
Junkers F 13da
Wingspan: 17.75 m (58 ft 2¾ in)
Length: 9.60 m (34 ft 6 in)
Wing area: 44.0 m² (473.61 sq ft)
Powerplant: 1 × 280-hp Junkers L2
Passenger capacity: 4
Empty weight: 1150 kg (2,535 lb)
Maximum take-off weight: 1730 kg (3,814 lb)
Maximum speed: 171 km/h (106 mph)
Cruising speed: 140 km/h (87 mph)
Service ceiling: 4000 m (31,120 ft)
Range: 949 km (590 miles)

Ford Tri-motor variants

Model 3-AT: original Stout Tri-motor prototype, destroyed 17 January 1926
Model 4-AT: first Ford Tri-motor; three J-4 Whirlwind radials and eight passengers
Model 4-AT-A: initial production model, similar to Model 4-AT; 14 built
Model 4-AT-B: increased span and J-5 Whirlwind radials; accommodation for two pilots and 12 passengers; 35 built
Model 4-AT-C: similar to the Model 4-AT-B but with 298-kW (400-hp) Wasp radial; 1 built
Model 4-AT-D: used wing similar to that of the Model 5-AT; total production was three, one having J-4 Whirlwind radial, another with two J-5 Whirlwind radials and one 298-kW (300-hp) J-6-9 Whirlwind radials, and the last with three J-6-9 Whirlwind radials
Model 4-AT-E: detail changes and three 298-kW (300-hp) J-6 Whirlwind radials; 24 built
Model 4-AT-F: one aircraft similar to the Model 4-AT-E and built in 1931
Model 5-AT-A: enlarged variant with three 313-kW (420-hp) Wasp radials; 3 built

Model 5-AT-B: new 15-seater of 1929 with three 313-kW (420-hp) Wasp C-1 or Wasp SC-1 radials; 42 built
Model 5-AT-C: improved 17-seat version; 48 built
Model 5-AT-D: increased-weight version with three 336-kW (450-hp) Wasp SC radials; 24 built
Model 6-AT-A: similar to the Model 5-AT-C but with J-6 Whirlwind radials; 3 built
Model 7-AT-A: rebuild of Model 6-AT-A with a nose-mounted 313-kW (420-hp) Wasp radial
Model 8-AT: single Model 5-AT-C converted as a freighter without wing-mounted engines
Model 9-AT: conversion of Model 4-AT-B with 224-kW (300-hp) Wasp Junior radials; 1 converted
Model 11-AT: one Model 4-AT-E rebuilt with 168-kW (225-hp) Packard DR-980 diesels
Model 13-A: conversion of one Model 5-AT-D with two J-6 Whirlwind radials and one 429-kW (575-hp) Cyclone radial
Model 14-A: one much larger aircraft of 1932 with two 533-kW (715-hp) and one 820-kW (1,100-hp) Hispano-Suiza engines; this 40-seater was completed but not flown
C-3: US Army no. 28-348, based on Model 4-AT-B
C-3A: US Army nos 29-220/226, seven aircraft with 175-kW (235-hp) R-790-3 Whirlwind radials
C-4: US Army no. 29-219, basically a Model 4-AT-B for military service
C-4A: US Army nos 31-401/404, four aircraft based on the Model 5-AT-D with 336-kW (450-hp) R-1340-11 radials
C-9: redesignation of all seven C-3As after the installation of 224-kW (300-hp) R-975-1 radials
XJR-1: US Navy no. A7526, based on Model 4-AT
JR-2: US Navy nos A8273/8274, two aircraft based on the Model 4-AT-E for the US Marine Corps
JR-3: US Navy nos A8457 and A8598/8599, three aircraft based on the Model 5-AT-C
RR-2: redesignation of JR-2
RR-3: redesignation of JR-3
RR-4: additional Model 5-AT-C with US Navy no. A8840
RR-5: US Navy nos 9205/9206, two aircraft based on the Model 5-AT-D, one of them delivered to the US Marine Corps
XB-906-1: single prototype (NX9652) for a bomber version with internal racks and two gunners' positions; crashed on 19 September 1931 killing Ford's chief test pilot, Leroy Manning

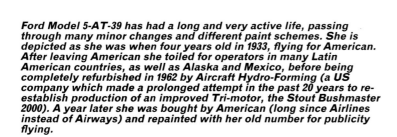

Ford Model 5-AT-39 has had a long and very active life, passing through many minor changes and different paint schemes. She is depicted as she was when four years old in 1933, flying for American. After leaving American she toiled for operators in many Latin American countries, as well as Alaska and Mexico, before being completely refurbished in 1962 by Aircraft Hydro-Forming (a US company which made a prolonged attempt in the past 20 years to re-establish production of an improved Tri-motor, the Stout Bushmaster 2000). A year later she was bought by American (long since Airlines instead of Airways) and repainted with her old number for publicity flying.

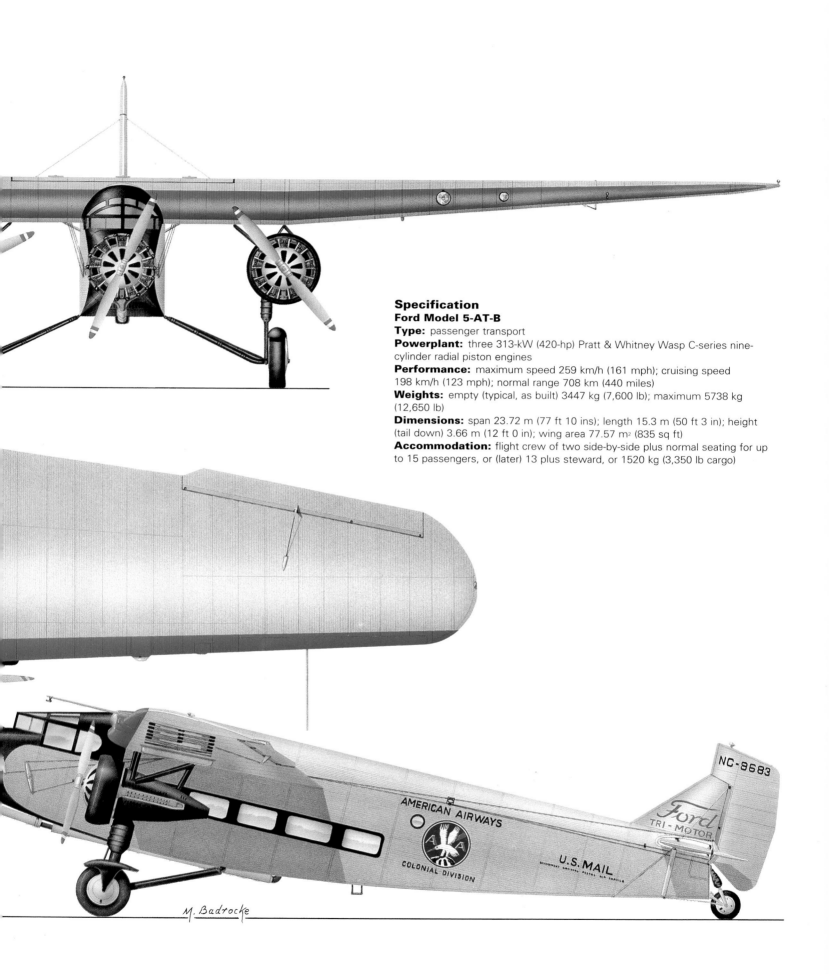

Specification
Ford Model 5-AT-B
Type: passenger transport
Powerplant: three 313-kW (420-hp) Pratt & Whitney Wasp C-series nine-cylinder radial piston engines
Performance: maximum speed 259 km/h (161 mph); cruising speed 198 km/h (123 mph); normal range 708 km (440 miles)
Weights: empty (typical, as built) 3447 kg (7,600 lb); maximum 5738 kg (12,650 lb)
Dimensions: span 23.72 m (77 ft 10 ins); length 15.3 m (50 ft 3 in); height (tail down) 3.66 m (12 ft 0 in); wing area 77.57 m² (835 sq ft)
Accommodation: flight crew of two side-by-side plus normal seating for up to 15 passengers, or (later) 13 plus steward, or 1520 kg (3,350 lb cargo)

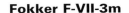

Fokker F-VII-3m

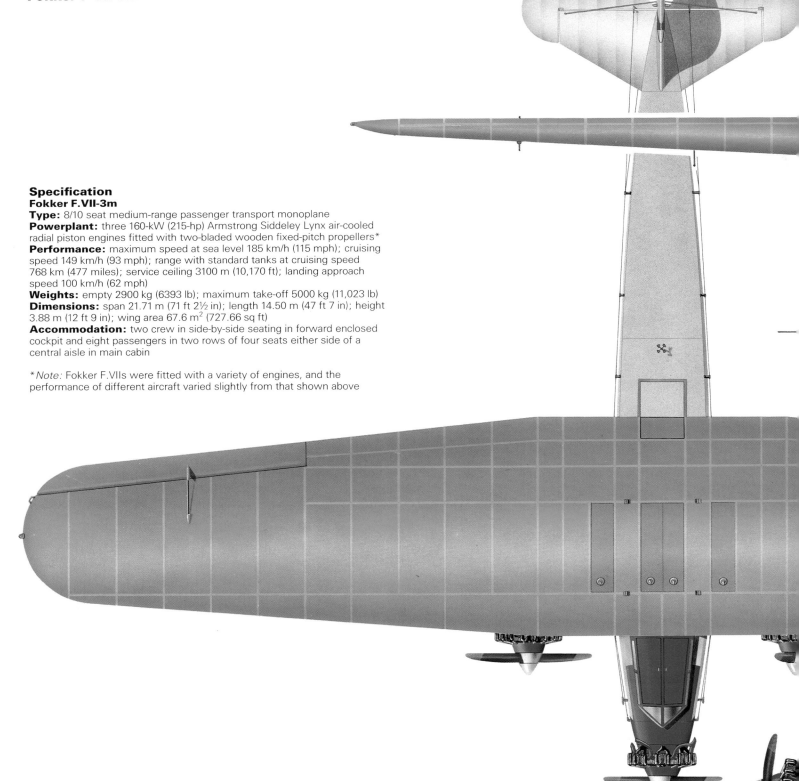

Specification
Fokker F.VII-3m
Type: 8/10 seat medium-range passenger transport monoplane
Powerplant: three 160-kW (215-hp) Armstrong Siddeley Lynx air-cooled radial piston engines fitted with two-bladed wooden fixed-pitch propellers*
Performance: maximum speed at sea level 185 km/h (115 mph); cruising speed 149 km/h (93 mph); range with standard tanks at cruising speed 768 km (477 miles); service ceiling 3100 m (10,170 ft); landing approach speed 100 km/h (62 mph)
Weights: empty 2900 kg (6393 lb); maximum take-off 5000 kg (11,023 lb)
Dimensions: span 21.71 m (71 ft 2½ in); length 14.50 m (47 ft 7 in); height 3.88 m (12 ft 9 in); wing area 67.6 m^2 (727.66 sq ft)
Accommodation: two crew in side-by-side seating in forward enclosed cockpit and eight passengers in two rows of four seats either side of a central aisle in main cabin

*Note: Fokker F.VIIs were fitted with a variety of engines, and the performance of different aircraft varied slightly from that shown above

This is the F.VII-3m commissioned by Mr R. Wanamaker for a special New York to Paris flight in 1927. Under the command of Commander Richard E. Byrd, this was intended to explore the possibilities of transatlantic commercial services. The aircraft was fitted with the long-span Fokker wing, long-range tanks and Wright J-5 Whirlwind engines together with an extended cockpit and an unusual forward-sloping windscreen. Named America, the Fokker finally departed with its four-man crew on 29 June 1927, but was forced to ditch in the English Channel near Le Havre when appalling weather conditions over Paris enveloped Le Bourget and the aircraft ran out of fuel after over 40 hours in the air.

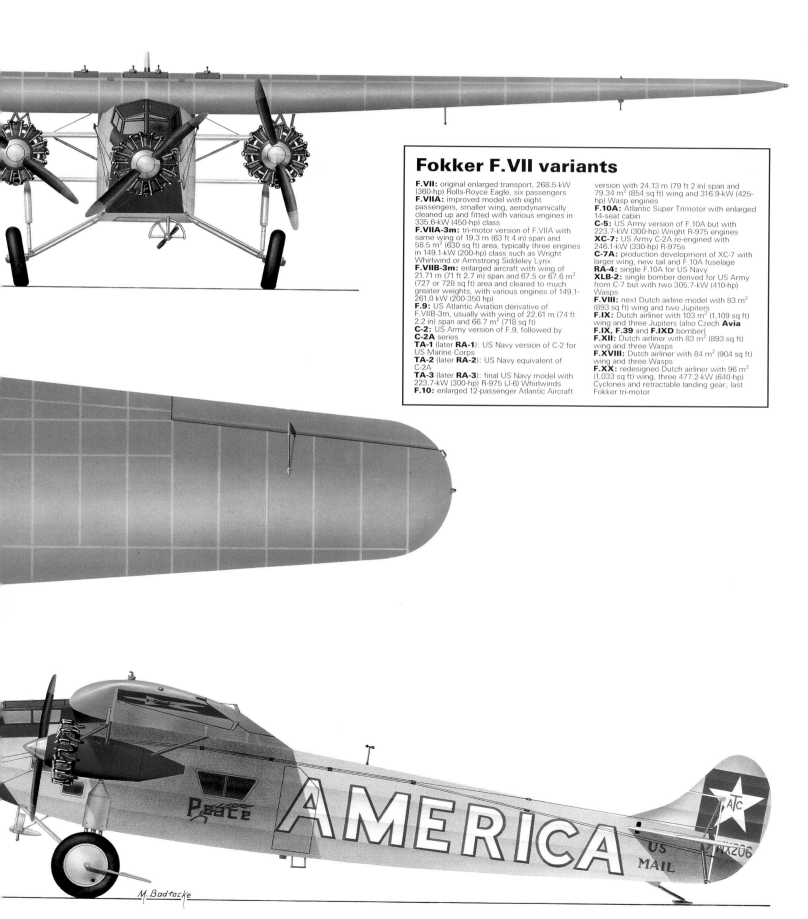

Fokker F.VII variants

F.VII: original enlarged transport, 268.5-kW (360-hp) Rolls-Royce Eagle, six passengers

F.VIIA: improved model with eight passengers, smaller wing, aerodynamically cleaned up and fitted with various engines in 335.6-kW (450-hp) class

F.VIIA-3m: tri-motor version of F.VIIA with same wing of 19.3 m (63 ft 4 in) span and 58.5 m² (630 sq ft) area, typically three engines in 149.1-kW (200-hp) class such as Wright Whirlwind or Armstrong Siddeley Lynx

F.VIIB-3m: enlarged aircraft with wing of 21.71 m (71 ft 2.7 in) span and 67.5 or 67.6 m² (727 or 728 sq ft) area and cleared to much greater weights, with various engines of 149.1-261.0 kW (200-350 hp)

F.9: US Atlantic Aviation derivative of F.VIIB-3m, usually with wing of 22.61 m (74 ft 2.2 in) span and 66.7 m² (718 sq ft)

C-2: US Army version of F.9, followed by **C-2A** series

TA-1 (later **RA-1**): US Navy version of C-2 for US Marine Corps

TA-2 (later **RA-2**): US Navy equivalent of C-2A

TA-3 (later **RA-3**): final US Navy model with 223.7-kW (300-hp) R-975 (J-6) Whirlwinds

F.10: enlarged 12-passenger Atlantic Aircraft

version with 24.13 m (79 ft 2 in) span and 79.34 m² (854 sq ft) wing and 316.9-kW (425-hp) Wasp engines

F.10A: Atlantic Super Trimotor with enlarged 14-seat cabin

C-5: US Army version of F.10A but with 223.7-kW (300-hp) Wright R-975 engines

XC-7: US Army C-2A re-engined with 246.1-kW (330-hp) R-975s

C-7A: production development of XC-7 with larger wing, new tail and F.10A fuselage

RA-4: single F.10A for US Navy

XLB-2: single bomber derived for US Army from C-7 but with two 305.7-kW (410-hp) Wasps

F.VIII: next Dutch airline model with 83 m² (893 sq ft) wing and two Jupiters

F.IX: Dutch airliner with 103 m² (1,109 sq ft) wing and three Jupiters (also Czech **Avia F.IX, F.39** and **F.IXD** bomber)

F.XII: Dutch airliner with 83 m² (893 sq ft) wing and three Wasps

F.XVIII: Dutch airliner with 84 m² (904 sq ft) wing and three Wasps

F.XX: redesigned Dutch airliner with 96 m² (1,033 sq ft) wing, three 477.2-kW (640-hp) Cyclones and retractable landing gear; last Fokker tri-motor

M. Bodtocke

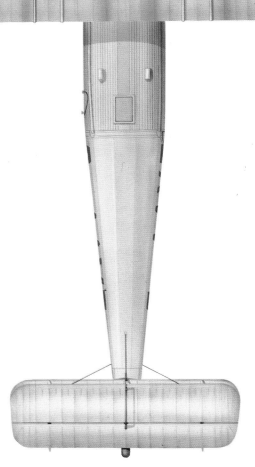

Specification
Handley Page H.P.42E
Wingspan: 39.62 m (130 ft)
Length: 28.1 m (92 ft)
Height: 8.23 m (27 ft)
Wing area: 278 m^2 (2,992 sq ft)
Powerplant: four 365-kW (490-hp) Bristol Jupiter XIF
Passenger capacity: 18-24
Empty weight: 8050 kg (17,750 lb)
Maximum take-off weight: 12,700 kg (28,000 lb)
Maximum cruising speed: 193 km/h (120 mph)
Service ceiling: 3800 m (12,450 ft)
Maximum range: 805 km (500 miles)

Specification
Handley Page H.P.42W
Wingspan: 39.62 m (130 ft)
Length: 28.1 m (92 ft)
Height: 8.23 m (27 ft)
Wing area: 278 m^2 (2,992 sq ft)
Powerplant: four 414-kW (555-hp) Bristol Jupiter XFBM
Passenger capacity: 38
Empty weight: 8050 kg (17,750 lb)
Maximum take-off weight: 13,760 kg (30,335 lb)
Maximum cruising speed: 204 km/h (126 mph)
Service ceiling: 3800 m (12,450 ft)
Maximum range: 480 km (300 miles)

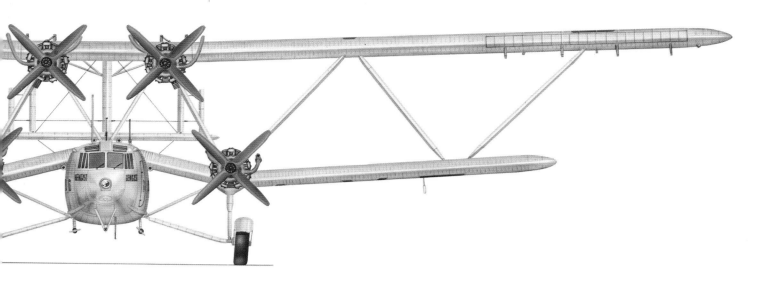

With its heavily-braced wings, undercarriage and tail unit, the H.P.42 had a 'built-in headwind', and indeed its cruising speed was very low even at the time of its introduction. Nevertheless, the type set new standards of reliability and safety which sleeker and more advanced competitors could not claim, while the inherent strength and quality of construction allowed them to survive many minor incidents throughout the 1930s. Among the many achievements of the 'flying bananas' (so called due to the kinked fuselage adopted to keep the passenger entry door as close to the ground as possible), it was the first commercial aircraft to fly 1,000,000 miles.

M. Badrocke

IMPERIAL AIRWAYS
LONDON

IMPERIAL AIRWAYS

ROYAL MAIL

G-AAXE

Dornier Do X

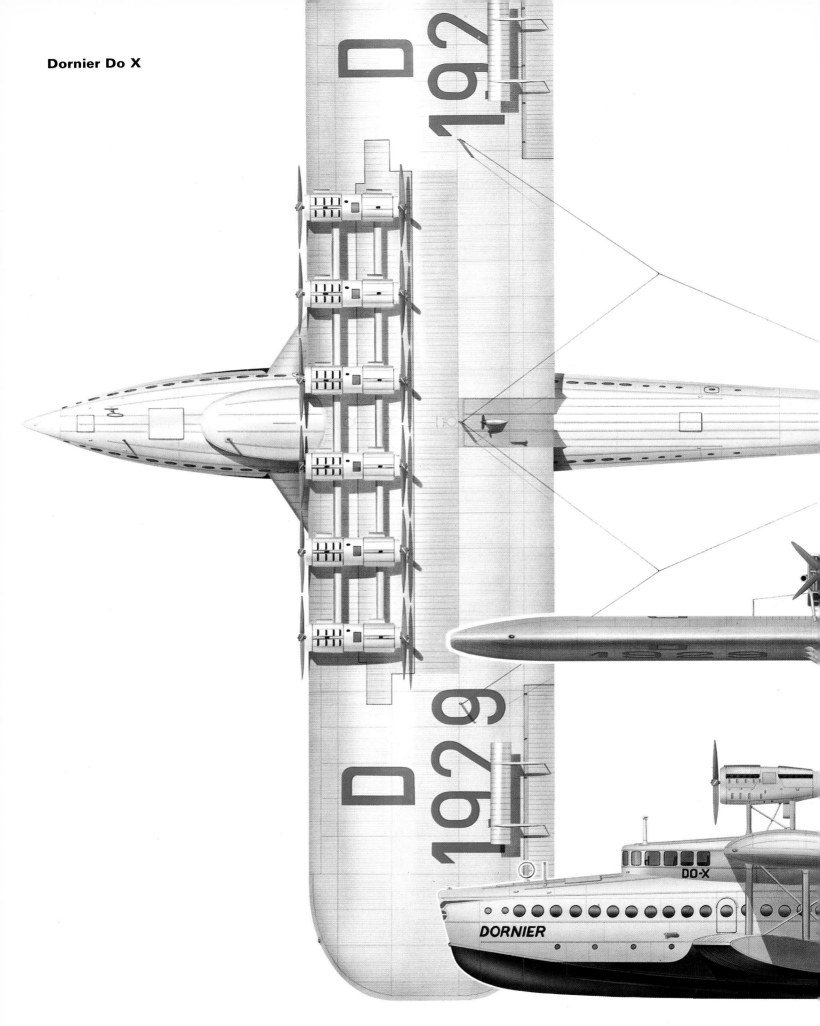

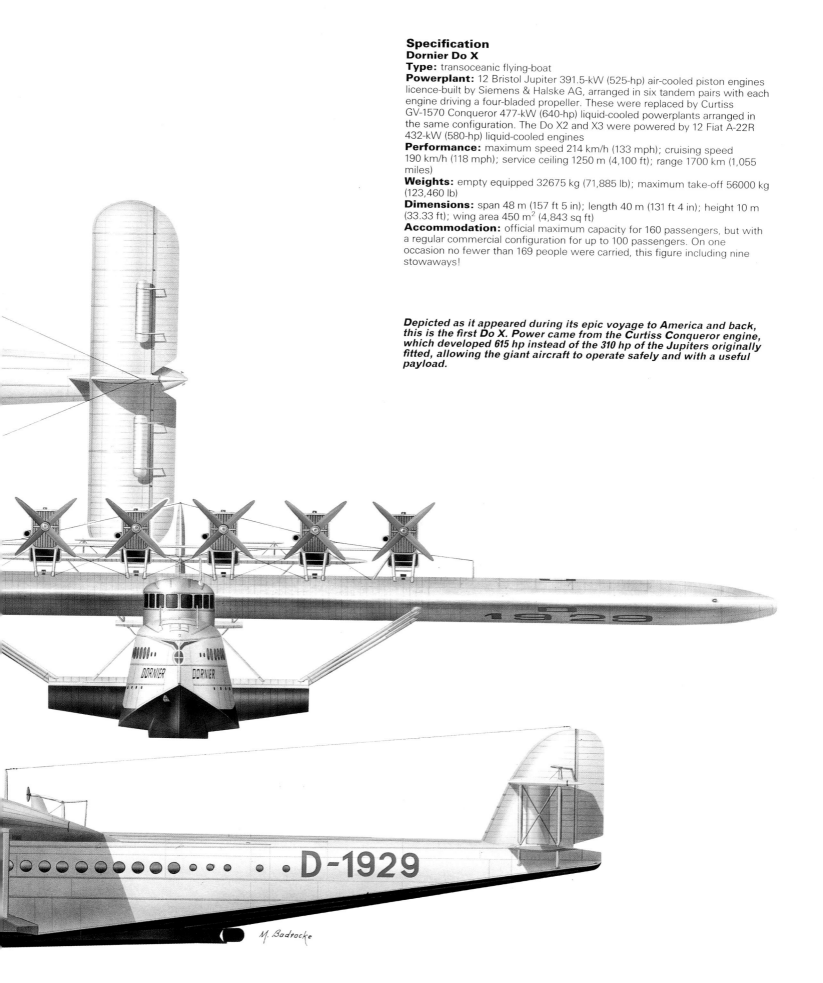

Specification
Dornier Do X

Type: transoceanic flying-boat

Powerplant: 12 Bristol Jupiter 391.5-kW (525-hp) air-cooled piston engines licence-built by Siemens & Halske AG, arranged in six tandem pairs with each engine driving a four-bladed propeller. These were replaced by Curtiss GV-1570 Conqueror 477-kW (640-hp) liquid-cooled powerplants arranged in the same configuration. The Do X2 and X3 were powered by 12 Fiat A-22R 432-kW (580-hp) liquid-cooled engines

Performance: maximum speed 214 km/h (133 mph); cruising speed 190 km/h (118 mph); service ceiling 1250 m (4,100 ft); range 1700 km (1,055 miles)

Weights: empty equipped 32675 kg (71,885 lb); maximum take-off 56000 kg (123,460 lb)

Dimensions: span 48 m (157 ft 5 in); length 40 m (131 ft 4 in); height 10 m (33.33 ft); wing area 450 m² (4,843 sq ft)

Accommodation: official maximum capacity for 160 passengers, but with a regular commercial configuration for up to 100 passengers. On one occasion no fewer than 169 people were carried, this figure including nine stowaways!

Depicted as it appeared during its epic voyage to America and back, this is the first Do X. Power came from the Curtiss Conqueror engine, which developed 615 hp instead of the 310 hp of the Jupiters originally fitted, allowing the giant aircraft to operate safely and with a useful payload.

Piper J-3C-65 Cub

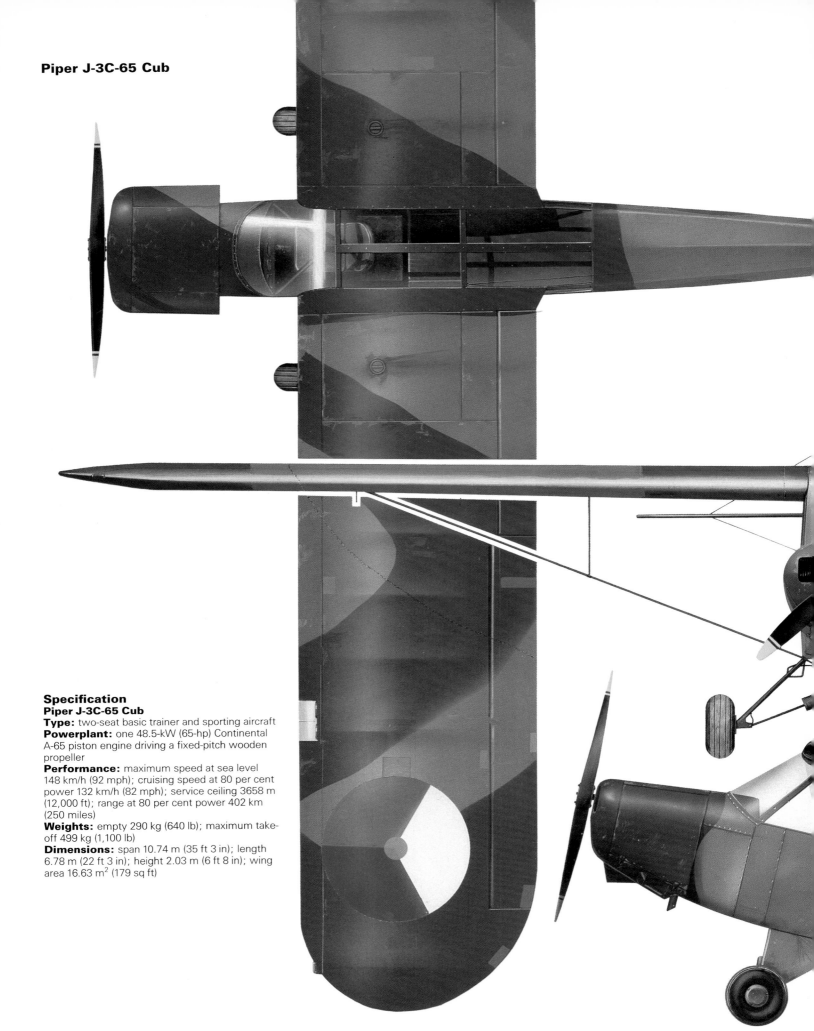

Specification
Piper J-3C-65 Cub
Type: two-seat basic trainer and sporting aircraft
Powerplant: one 48.5-kW (65-hp) Continental A-65 piston engine driving a fixed-pitch wooden propeller
Performance: maximum speed at sea level 148 km/h (92 mph); cruising speed at 80 per cent power 132 km/h (82 mph); service ceiling 3658 m (12,000 ft); range at 80 per cent power 402 km (250 miles)
Weights: empty 290 kg (640 lb); maximum take-off 499 kg (1,100 lb)
Dimensions: span 10.74 m (35 ft 3 in); length 6.78 m (22 ft 3 in); height 2.03 m (6 ft 8 in); wing area 16.63 m^2 (179 sq ft)

Piper Cub variants

E-2: original two-seat parasol-wing monoplane with 27.6-kW (37-hp) Continental A-40 engine
F-2: E-2 powered by 29.8-kW (40-hp) Aeromarine AR3-40 engine
G-2: experimental E-2 with Taylor engine
H-2: E-2 with 29.8-kW (40-hp) Szekely engine
J-2: E-2 with built-up rear fuselage, enclosed cabin and rounded wing and tail surfaces
J-3C-40: J-2 with stronger airframe and detail improvements
J-3C-50: J-3 with 37.3-kW (50-hp) Continental A-50 engine
J-3C-65: J-3 with 48.5-kW (65-hp) Continental A-65 engine
J-3F-50: J-3 with 37.3-kW (50-hp) Franklin 4AC-150 engine
J-3F-65: J-3 with 48.5-kW (65-hp) Franklin 4AC-176 engine
J-3P-50: J-3 with 37.3-kW (50-hp) Lenape LM-3 Papoose engine
J-3L-50: J-3 with 37.3-kW (50-hp) Lycoming O-145 engine
J-3L-65: J-3 with 48.5-kW (65-hp) Lycoming O-145-B engine
J-4 Cub Coupe: J-3 with wider fuselage and side-by-side seating; powered by 37.3-kW (50-hp) Continental A-50 engine
J-4A: J-4 with 48.5-kW (65-hp) Continental A-65 engine
J-4B: J-4 with 48.5-kW (65-hp) Franklin 4AC-176-B2 engine
J-4F: J-4 with 48.5-kW (65-hp) Lycoming O-145-B1 engine
J-5A Cub Cruiser: J-4 with wider three-seat fuselage and enlarged fin; powered by 55.9-kW (75-hp) Continental A-75-8 engine
J-5B: J-5A with 55.9-kW (75-hp) Lycoming GO-145-C2 engine
J-5C: J-5A with 74.6-kW (100-hp) Lycoming O-235-C engine
PA-11 Cub Special: improved J-3C-65 with stronger airframe, fully enclosed engine cowling and divided landing gear
PA-18-95: improved PA-11 with strengthened airframe and Continental C-90 engine
PA-18-105: PA-18 with 80.5-kW (108-hp) Lycoming O-235 engine
PA-18-125: PA-18 with 93.2-kW (125-hp) Lycoming O-290 engine
PA-18-135: PA-18 with 100.7-kW (135-hp) O-290 engine

PA-18-150: PA-18 with 111.9-kW (150-hp) Lycoming O-320 engine
PA-18A: special agricultural PA-18 with 100.7- or 111.9-kW (135- or 150-hp) engine
O-59: military version of Cub J-3C-65; redesignated L-4
O-59A: O-59 with enlarged rear cabin glazing; became L-4A
L-4: revised designation for O-59
L-4A: revised designation for O-59A
L-4B: L-4A with 48.5-kW (65-hp) O-170-3 engine and no radio
L-4C: impressed Model J-3L-65
L-4D: impressed Model J-3F-65
L-4E: impressed Model J-4E-75
L-4F: impressed Model J-5A
L-4G: impressed Model J-5B
L-4H: L-4B with fixed-pitch propeller and detail changes
L-4J: L-4H with variable-pitch propeller
UC-83: Model J-5A impressed in Panama
UC-83A: Model J-3L-65A impressed in Panama
UC-83B: Model J-4A impressed in Panama
TG-8: three-seat training glider based on J-3 airframe
HE-1: ambulance version of J-5C with removable fuselage decking
AE-1: revised designation for HE-1; used by US Navy
XLNP-1: US Navy version of TG-8
NE-1: US Navy version of L-4 with 48.5-kW (65-hp) O-170-2 engine
NE-2: NE-1 with minor alterations to equipment
L-14: three-seat version of L-4; five prototypes only
L-18B: military version of PA-11-95 for Turkish army
L-18C: PA-18-95 for US Army and MAP delivery
YL-21: PA-18 powered by 100.7-kW (135-hp) engine
L-21A: PA-18 powered by 93.2-kW (125-hp) O-290-11 engine
L-21B: L-21A with 100.7-kW (135-hp) O-290-D2 engine
U-7: revised designation for L-21B

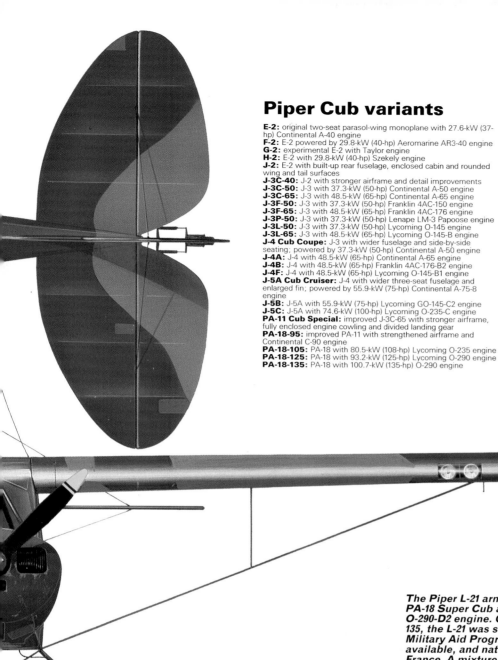

The Piper L-21 army co-operation aircraft was developed from the PA-18 Super Cub and powered by a 101-kW (135-hp) Continental O-290-D2 engine. Of very similar layout to the commercial Super Cub 135, the L-21 was supplied to various NATO military forces under the Military Aid Program. The lower-powered L-18 was also made available, and nations using these types included Belgium, Italy and France. A mixture of L-18Cs, L-21As and L-21Bs was provided to the Dutch army and operated by Nos 298, 299 and 300 Squadrons. Deliveries started in February 1955, and 34 aircraft were written off in service. This particular machine was an L-21B with No. 299 Squadron, based at Deelen. Many military Super Cubs were sold to civil users after their service lives were over.

21

The heart of the He 70's remarkable speed performance lay in its shape, and this represents one of the high points in the art of aeronautical design. Everything about the aircraft suggested speed, and it delivered the goods although it was not very manoeuvrable. For Lufthansa in the mid-1930s it was used mainly on internal routes, linking major cities with high-priority passengers. It also took the mail, even as far as Seville on the South American route. Luftwaffe interest was naturally high, and they received three early aircraft destined for Lufthansa. This is one of them, originally built as an He 70B but completed as an He 70C military communications aircraft.

Specification
Heinkel He 70G-1
Wingspan: 14.78 m (48 ft 6 in)
Length: 11.48 m (37 ft 7 in)
Height: 3.1 m (10 ft 2 in)
Wing area: 36.5 m² (393 sq ft)
Powerplant: one 469-kW (630-hp) BMW VI V-12 piston engine
Passenger capacity: five
Empty weight: 2300 kg (5071 lb)
Maximum take-off weight: 3310 kg (7297 lb)
Maximum speed: 355 km/h (221 mph)
Cruising speed: 310 km/h (193 mph)
Service ceiling: 6000 m (19,685 ft)
Maximum range: 800 km (497 miles)

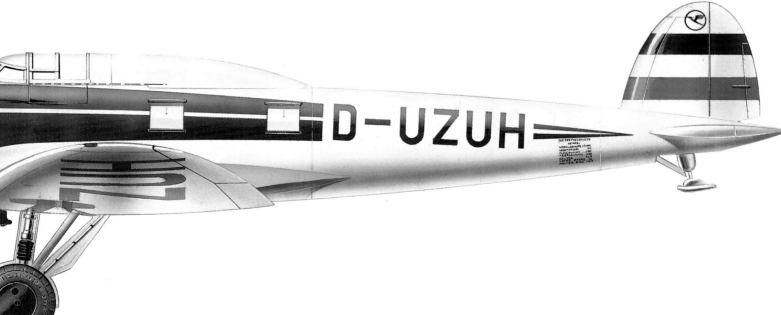

Short S.21 Maia/Mercury

Short Civil Flying Boats variants

S.20 Mercury: upper component of Short-Mayo Composite. Fitted with sealed float tanks for long-distance record flight; one built

S.21 Maia: lower component of Short-Mayo Composite. Similar to S.23 except for enlarged wing (same span), enlarged wing floats, tail and tailplane. Upswept hull positioned tailplane higher to counteract effects of upper component when fitted. Large pylon structure on back to supprt *Mercury*; one built

S.23 'C-class' Empire Boat: basis of Short flying boat family. Development batch of two, including one long-range variant with extra tankage. Imperial production batches of 12 and 14. Three ordered for QANTAS

S.25 Sunderland: military anti-submarine aircraft based on C-class design. Several **Sunderland Mk IIIs** used by BOAC for wartime services with rudimentary seating; 19 conversions for BOAC, four for RNZAF Flying Boat Transport Flight, (post-war) three for CAUSA (Uruguay), two for Aerolineas Argentinas, three for Trans-Oceanic Airways

S.26 'G-class': larger version of S.23 with revised low-drag hull and lower cockpit profile. Named *Golden Hind* class. During World War II fitted with ASV radar and tail turret for RAF use. These were removed after the war for BOAC service, resulting in a lengthened tail cone being fitted; three built for Imperial

S.30 'C-class' Empire Boat: improved version of S.23 with Perseus XIIC sleeve-valve engines, strengthening to raise take-off weight and tankage for 2415 km (1,500 miles). Some equipped for mid-air refuelling from Handley Page Harrows; nine built for Imperial and QANTAS

S.33 'C-class' Empire Boat: further improved variant ordered as attrition replacement for Imperial Airways. Strengthened hulls and Pegasus XI engines, later re-engined with Pegasus XXIIs and a corresponding rise in take-off weight to 24040 kg (53,000 lb); two completed and one partially built

Hythe: Sunderland Mk IIIs fitted with full airliner standard interiors. Initial version had 16 seats, but later a promenade deck or 8 extra seats were added

Sandringham Mk 1: ex-BOAC Sunderland Mk III fitted with low drag nose and pointed tailcone. Furnished internally for 24 day or 16 night passengers with dining saloon and cocktail bar; one conversion for BOAC

Sandringham Mk 2: local route version for Dodero, seating for 45; three conversions from Sunderlands

Sandringham Mk 3: long range version for Dodero, seating for 21 with dining saloon and bar; two conversions from Sunderlands

Sandringham Mk 4: TEAL version with accommodation for 30 passengers; four conversions

Sandringham Mk 5: known as the *Plymouth* class. Accommodation for 22 day or 16 night passengers on one deck only. Powered by Pratt & Whitney R-1830-90D Twin Wasps; nine Sunderland conversions for BOAC

Sandringham Mk 6: furnished for 37 day pasengers on two decks and equipped with ASV 6C radar and other equipment for northern flying; five conversions for DNL

Sandringham Mk 7: improved aircraft with 30 seats for BOAC Far East services; three conversions

'Near-Sandringham': one ex-RNZAF Sunderland converted for Ansett to Sandringham standard in Australia in 1963 but with different nose profile. Accommodation for 43

Solent Mk 1: proposed civil version of Seaford (following BOAC use of the second-production aircraft)

S.45A Solent Mk 2: the Solent 1s ordered by BOAC were changed during construction to Mk 2, with day interior for 34 passengers. Hercules 637 engines; 12 built

Solent Mk 3: redundant Seafords modified to airliner standard with seating for 39; six conversions for BOAC and one for Aquila

Solent Mk 4: heavier version with Hercules 733 engines and increased fuel tankage. Furnished for 44 passengers; four for TEAL

Specification
Short S.21 *Maia*

Type: launch aircraft for *Mercury* mailplane

Powerplant: four Bristol Pegasus radial engines

Performance: maximum speed 322 km/h (200 mph); service ceiling 6100 m (20,000 ft); range 1360 km (850 miles)

Weights: empty 11234 kg (24,745 lb); all-up (solo) 17252 kg (38,000 lb); max (for Composite launch) 12580 kg (27,700 lb)

Dimensions: span 34.70 m (114 ft); length 25.9 m (84 ft 11 in); wing area 162.5 m² (1,750 sq ft)

Specification
Short S.20 *Mercury* (record-breaking configuration)

Type: long range twin-float mailplane

Powerplant: four Napier-Halford Rapier VI inline engines

Performance: maximum speed 339 km/h (212 mph); range from Composite launch 9820 km (6,100 miles)

Weights: empty 4614 kg (10,163 lb); all-up (solo) 7030 kg (15,500 lb); all-up (record) 12160 kg (26,800 lb)

Dimensions: span 22.20 m (73 ft); length 15.50 m (51 ft); wing area 56.8 m² (611 sq ft)

The Short-Mayo Composite was a considerable success for its day, and provided one of the more remarkable chapters in commercial aviation history. The S.21 Maia first flew on 27 July 1937, to be followed by the S.20 Mercury on 5 September the same year. On 20 January 1938, the Composite flew for the first time, and on 6 February achieved the first, uneventful, separation. After Ministry trials at Felixstowe, the first big test for the concept came on 21 July, when Mercury was launched over Foynes, Ireland, with a load of newspapers, newsreels and press photographs. Just over 20 hours later it arrived at Boucherville, Montreal, with over 80 gallons of fuel remaining. After flying on to New York, it returned in triumph to England in shorter hops. With this success, the Composite was authorised to attempt a seaplane distance record. Launched from Dundee on 6 October, the modified Mercury flew south for over 42 hours, falling short of its planned destination of Cape Town due to numerous adversities, but gaining the straight-line distance record with 5,997.5 miles, landing on the Orange River. A few services were flown for BOAC, and with the beginning of war the Composite was split, the upper section passing into RAF hands. Both components were destroyed in 1941, Mercury at the hands of scrappers at Rochester and Maia by Luftwaffe bombs at Poole.

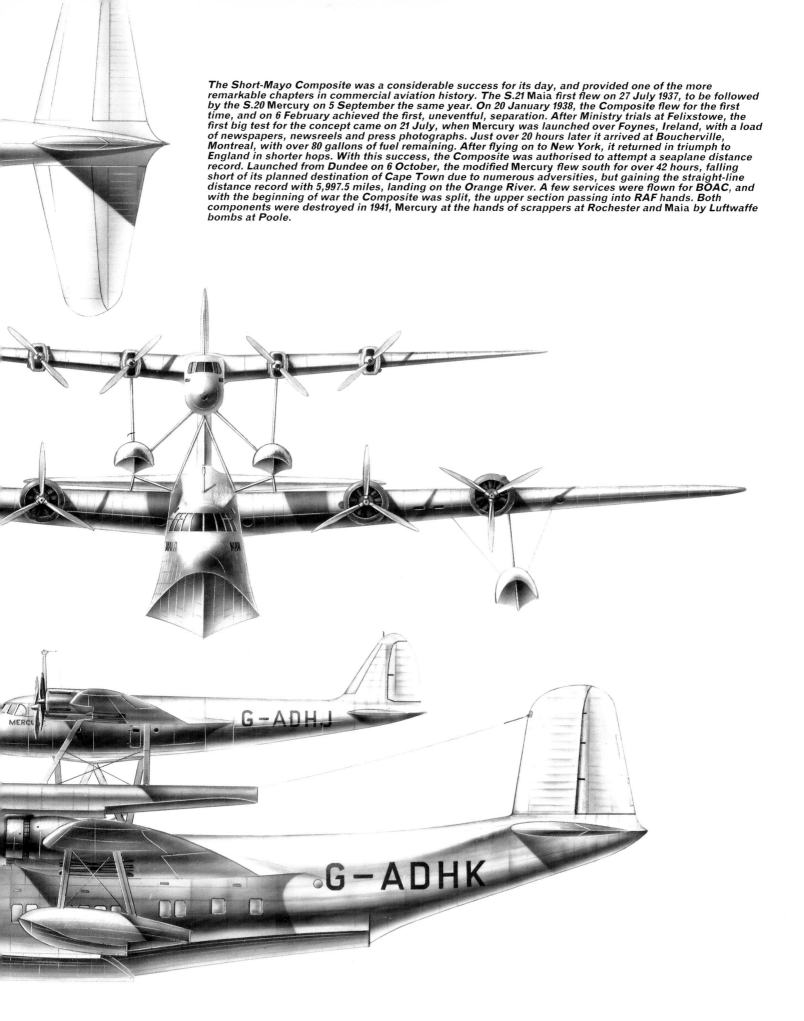

Lockheed Model 14 Super Electra

Specification
Lockheed Model 14 Super Electra
Type: medium-range airliner/executive transport
Powerplant: two Wright SGR-1820-F62 Cyclone radial engines rated at 671.4 kW (900 hp) each
Performance: maximum speed 402 km/h (250 mph); normal cruising speed 367 km/h (228 mph); service ceiling 7468 m (24,500 ft); maximum range 2558 km (1,590 miles); range with maximum payload 1368 km (850 miles)
Weights: empty 4876 kg (10,750 lb); maximum take-off 7938 kg (17,500 lb)
Dimensions: wing span 19.96 m (65 ft 6 in); length 13.51 m (44 ft 4 in); height 3.48 m (11 ft 5 in); wing area 51.19 m² (551 sq ft)
Accommodation: normal flight crew of two; seating for 10-14 passengers

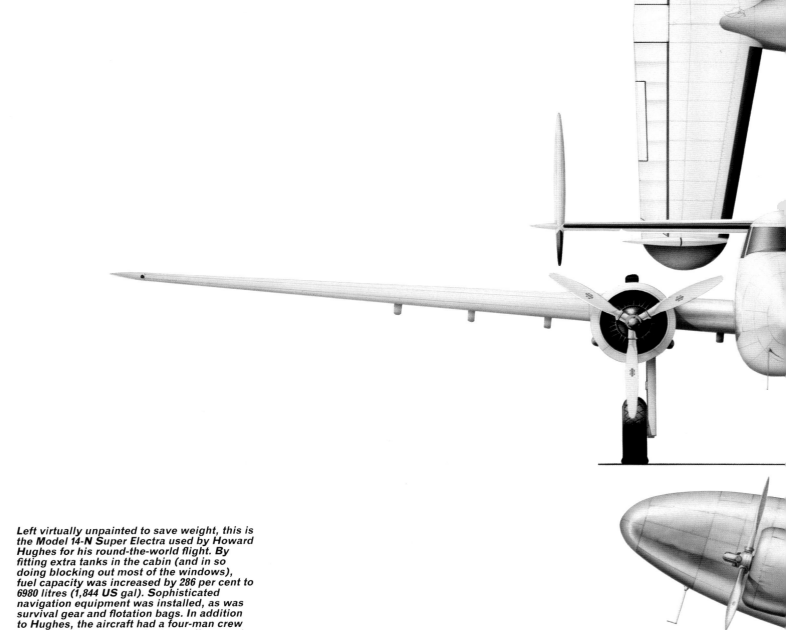

Left virtually unpainted to save weight, this is the Model 14-N Super Electra used by Howard Hughes for his round-the-world flight. By fitting extra tanks in the cabin (and in so doing blocking out most of the windows), fuel capacity was increased by 286 per cent to 6980 litres (1,844 US gal). Sophisticated navigation equipment was installed, as was survival gear and flotation bags. In addition to Hughes, the aircraft had a four-man crew comprising co-pilot, navigator, radio operator and flight engineer. The trip covered some 23611 km (14,672 miles) at an average speed of 331.6 km/h (206.1 mph)

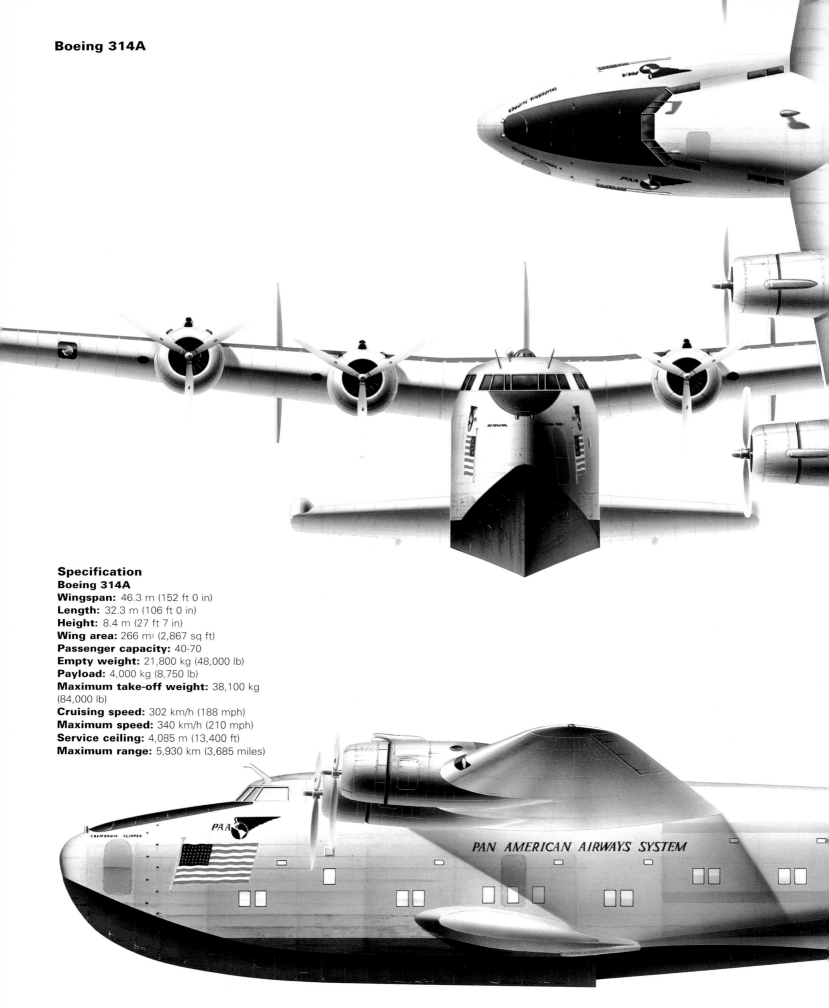

Boeing 314A

Specification
Boeing 314A
Wingspan: 46.3 m (152 ft 0 in)
Length: 32.3 m (106 ft 0 in)
Height: 8.4 m (27 ft 7 in)
Wing area: 266 m² (2,867 sq ft)
Passenger capacity: 40-70
Empty weight: 21,800 kg (48,000 lb)
Payload: 4,000 kg (8,750 lb)
Maximum take-off weight: 38,100 kg (84,000 lb)
Cruising speed: 302 km/h (188 mph)
Maximum speed: 340 km/h (210 mph)
Service ceiling: 4,085 m (13,400 ft)
Maximum range: 5,930 km (3,685 miles)

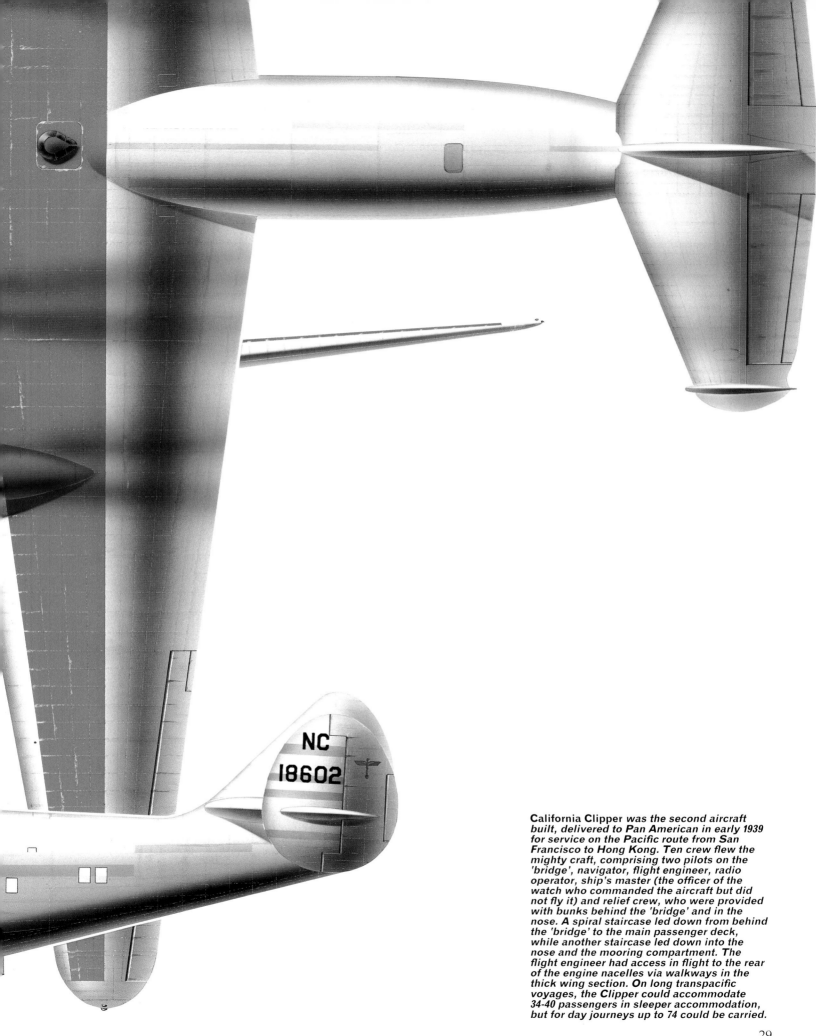

California Clipper *was the second aircraft built, delivered to* Pan American *in early 1939 for service on the Pacific route from* San Francisco *to* Hong Kong. *Ten crew flew the mighty craft, comprising two pilots on the 'bridge', navigator, flight engineer, radio operator, ship's master (the officer of the watch who commanded the aircraft but did not fly it) and relief crew, who were provided with bunks behind the 'bridge' and in the nose. A spiral staircase led down from behind the 'bridge' to the main passenger deck, while another staircase led down into the nose and the mooring compartment. The flight engineer had access in flight to the rear of the engine nacelles via walkways in the thick wing section. On long transpacific voyages, the* Clipper *could accommodate 34-40 passengers in sleeper accommodation, but for day journeys up to 74 could be carried.*

Junkers G 38ce

The second G 38 was the longer-lived, and wore three different registrations. It first flew in 1932, certificated in June of that year and entered Lufthansa service in July. Wearing the registration D-2500, it saw service on various routes from Berlin, including Scandinavia, Vienna-Rome, Amsterdam-London, Danzig-Königsberg and routes within Germany. In 1934 a new registration scheme saw it christened D-APIS, and Lufthansa services continued until 1939. Impressed in September, it served with KGrzbV 172 wearing the code GF-GG.

Specification
Junkers G 38ce

Type: four-engined passenger transport

Powerplant: four Junkers L 88a vee-12 liquid-cooled engines, rated at 750 hp each, driving wooden four-bladed propellers of 4.50 m (14 ft 9 in) diameter

Performance: maximum speed 210 km/h (130 mph); cruising speed 185 km/h (115 mph); service ceiling 3100 m (10,170 ft); rate of climb at sea level 177 m (580 ft per minute); time to 3000 m (9,842 ft) 34 minutes; endurance at cruising speed 10 hours; take-off run 400 m (1,312 ft); landing run 260 m (853 ft); landing speed 93 km/h (58 mph)

Weights: empty 16400 kg (36,156 lb); maximum take-off 23000 kg (50,706 lb); fuel load 2610 kg (5,754 lb)

Dimensions: wing span 44 m (144 ft 4¼ in); length 23.2 m (76 ft 1¼ in); height 7.2 m (23 ft 9 in); wing area 305 m² (3,283 sq ft)

Accommodation: crew of seven (two pilots, captain, radio operator, two engineers, steward); normal seating for 32-34 passengers

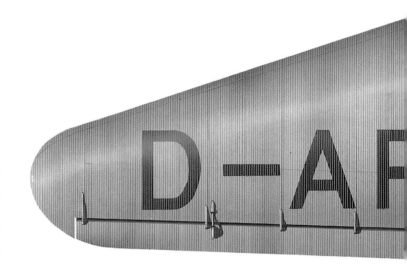

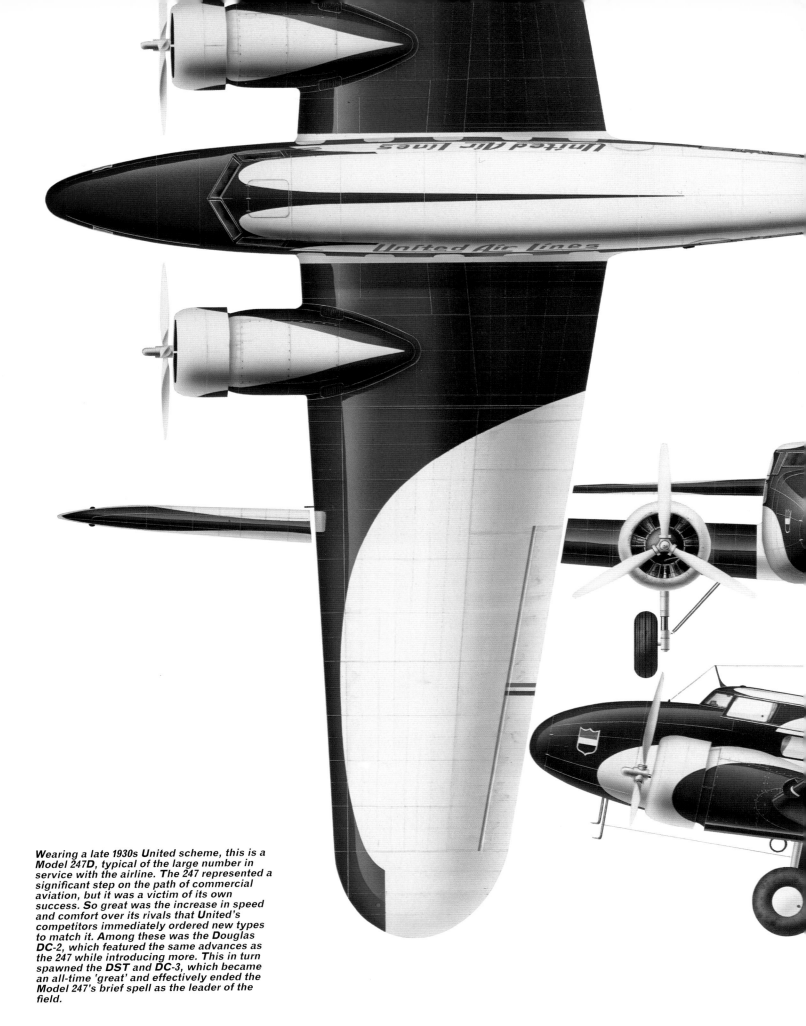

Wearing a late 1930s United scheme, this is a Model 247D, typical of the large number in service with the airline. The 247 represented a significant step on the path of commercial aviation, but it was a victim of its own success. So great was the increase in speed and comfort over its rivals that United's competitors immediately ordered new types to match it. Among these was the Douglas DC-2, which featured the same advances as the 247 while introducing more. This in turn spawned the DST and DC-3, which became an all-time 'great' and effectively ended the Model 247's brief spell as the leader of the field.

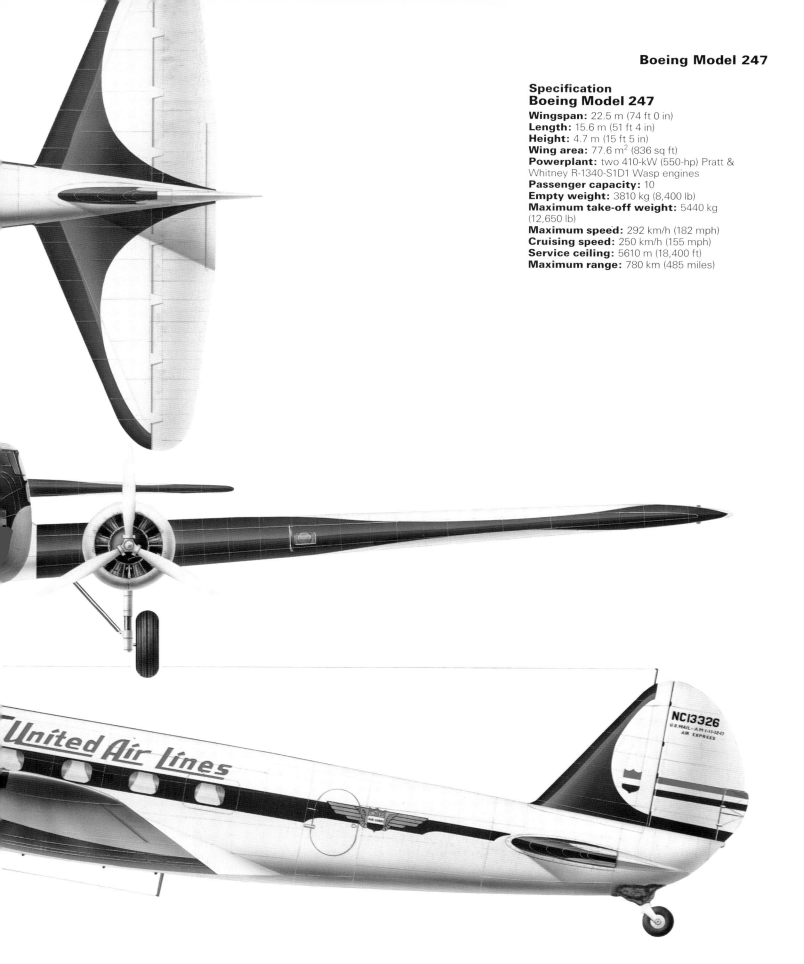

Specification
Boeing Model 247
Wingspan: 22.5 m (74 ft 0 in)
Length: 15.6 m (51 ft 4 in)
Height: 4.7 m (15 ft 5 in)
Wing area: 77.6 m² (836 sq ft)
Powerplant: two 410-kW (550-hp) Pratt &
Whitney R-1340-S1D1 Wasp engines
Passenger capacity: 10
Empty weight: 3810 kg (8,400 lb)
Maximum take-off weight: 5440 kg
(12,650 lb)
Maximum speed: 292 km/h (182 mph)
Cruising speed: 250 km/h (155 mph)
Service ceiling: 5610 m (18,400 ft)
Maximum range: 780 km (485 miles)

Lockheed Vega 5C/Sirius DL-2/Orion 9

Specification
Lockheed Vega 5C
Wingspan: 12.5 m (41 ft)
Length: 8.38 m (27 ft 6 in)
Height: 2.6 m (8 ft 6 in)
Wing area: 25.5 m^2 (275 sq ft)
Powerplant: one 336-kW (450-hp) Pratt & Whitney Wasp radial engine
Passenger capacity: 6
Empty weight: 1163 kg (2,565 lb)
Maximum take-off weight: 2041 kg (4,500 lb)
Maximum speed: 298 km/h (185 mph)
Cruising speed: 266 km/h (165 mph)
Service ceiling: 5791 m (19,000 ft)
Maximum range: 1167 km (725 miles)

Specification
Lockheed Sirius DL-2
Wingspan: 13 m (42 ft 10 in)
Length: 8.5 m (27 ft 10 in)
Height: 2.8 m (9 ft 2 in)
Wing area: 27.3 m^2 (294 sq ft)
Powerplant: one 313-kW (420-hp) Pratt & Whitney Wasp C radial engine
Passenger capacity: 1
Empty weight: 1342 kg (2,958 lb)
Maximum take-off weight: 2345 kg (5,170 lb)
Maximum speed: 282 km/h (175 mph)
Cruising speed: 233 km/h (145 mph)
Service ceiling: 5486 m (18,000 ft)
Maximum range: 1569 km (975 miles)

Specification
Lockheed Orion 9
Wingspan: 13 m (42 ft 9¼ in)
Length: 8.4 m (27 ft 8 in)
Height: 2.9 m (9 ft 8 in)
Wing area: 27.3 m^2 (294 sq ft)
Powerplant: one 306/313-kW (410/420-hp) Pratt & Whitney Wasp A/C radial engine
Passenger capacity: 6
Empty weight: 1551 kg (3,420 lb)
Maximum take-off weight: 2359 kg (5,200 lb)
Maximum speed: 354 km/h (220 mph)
Cruising speed: 282 km/h (175 mph)
Service ceiling: 6706 m (22,000 ft)
Maximum range: 1207 km (750 miles)

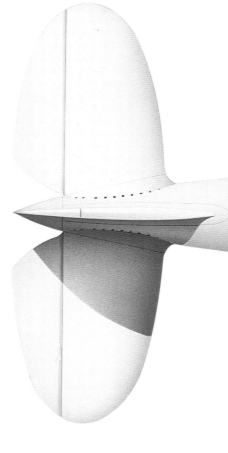

Rapidly becoming one of the most famous individual aircraft in the world, the 'Winnie Mae' was the Model 5B Vega used by Wiley Post to win the National Air Races, followed by a round-the-world record flight, then the first ever solo circumnavigation, and finally a series of high-altitude and transcontinental record attempts. Certainly Post's efforts proved conclusively the intrinsic value of the Jack Northrop design. Thankfully the 'Winnie Mae' was spared from an untimely fate, and is now one of the key exhibits in the National Air and Space Museum in Washington. Post was not so lucky, being killed at the start of his third circumnavigation attempt.

de Havilland D.H.89A

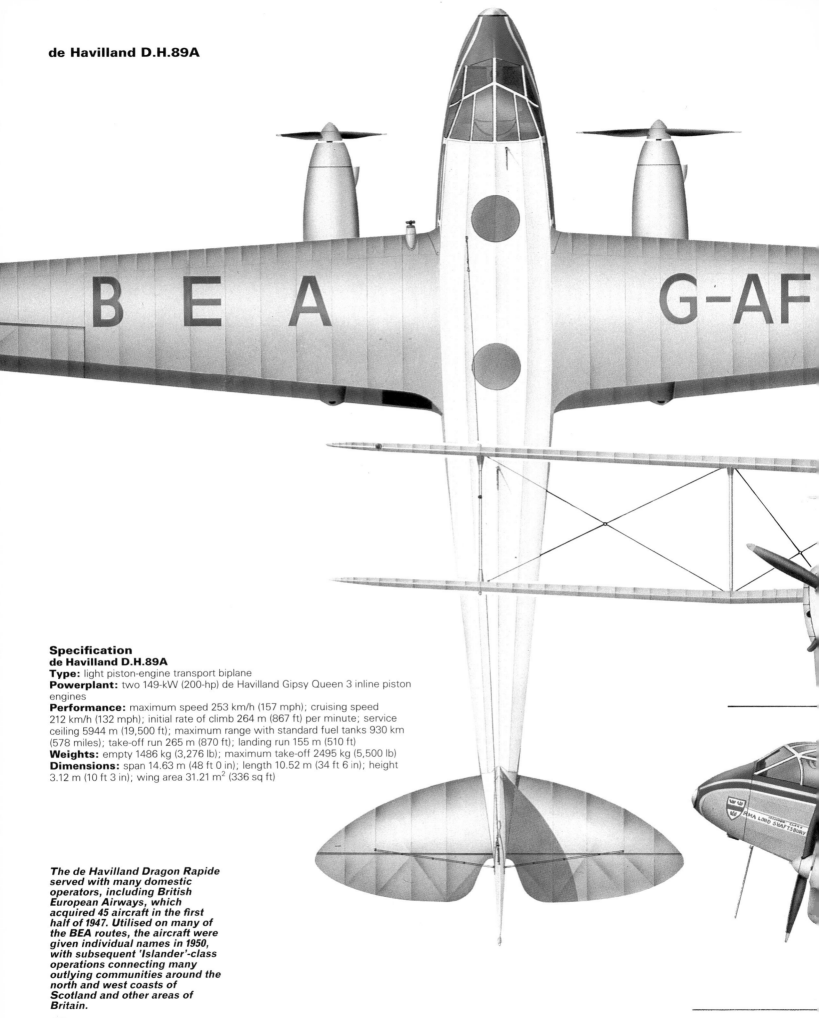

BEA **G-AF**

Specification
de Havilland D.H.89A
Type: light piston-engine transport biplane
Powerplant: two 149-kW (200-hp) de Havilland Gipsy Queen 3 inline piston engines
Performance: maximum speed 253 km/h (157 mph); cruising speed 212 km/h (132 mph); initial rate of climb 264 m (867 ft) per minute; service ceiling 5944 m (19,500 ft); maximum range with standard fuel tanks 930 km (578 miles); take-off run 265 m (870 ft); landing run 155 m (510 ft)
Weights: empty 1486 kg (3,276 lb); maximum take-off 2495 kg (5,500 lb)
Dimensions: span 14.63 m (48 ft 0 in); length 10.52 m (34 ft 6 in); height 3.12 m (10 ft 3 in); wing area 31.21 m² (336 sq ft)

The de Havilland Dragon Rapide served with many domestic operators, including British European Airways, which acquired 45 aircraft in the first half of 1947. Utilised on many of the BEA routes, the aircraft were given individual names in 1950, with subsequent 'Islander'-class operations connecting many outlying communities around the north and west coasts of Scotland and other areas of Britain.

de Havilland Dragon and Dragon Rapide variants

D.H.84 Dragon I: six-passenger cabin biplane powered by two 96.9-kW (130-hp) Gipsy Major 1 piston engines

D.H.84 Dragon II: Dragon 1 with framed cabin windows, faired-in landing gear legs and 9-km/h (6-mph) maximum speed improvement

D.H.86 Express: scaled-up version of D.H.84 with four Gipsy Six engines and increased passenger capacity

D.H.89 Dragon Six: developed Dragon with new, non-folding wings and construction based on D.H.86 Express; powered by 149-kW (200-hp) Gipsy Six engines

D.H.89A Dragon Rapide: D.H.89 fitted with split trailing-edge flaps; some D.H.89s retrospectively modified

D.H.89B Dominie Mk 1: D.H.89A for RAF as W/T and navigation trainer

D.H.89B Dominie Mk 2: communications transport version of DH.89B for RAF

D.H.89A Rapide Mk 2: post-war civil Rapide with six passenger seats, pilot and radio operator

D.H.89A Rapide Mk 3: post-war Rapide with eight passenger seats and pilot

D.H.89A Rapide Mk 4: D.H.89A converted with 149-kW (200-hp) Gipsy Queen Mk 2 engines fitted with constant-speed propellers

D.H.89A Rapide Mk 5: Rapide converted with Gipsy Queen 3MVP engines and manually operated variable-pitch propellers

D.H.89A Rapide Mk 6: Rapide fitted with Fairey X5 fixed-pitch metal propellers

D.H.89M: military version of D.H.89A with extended fin, twin nose-mounted Vickers Mk V guns and open mid-upper turret with one Lewis Mk III gun on ring mounting

G-AFEZ

ROYAL MAIL

M. Badrocke

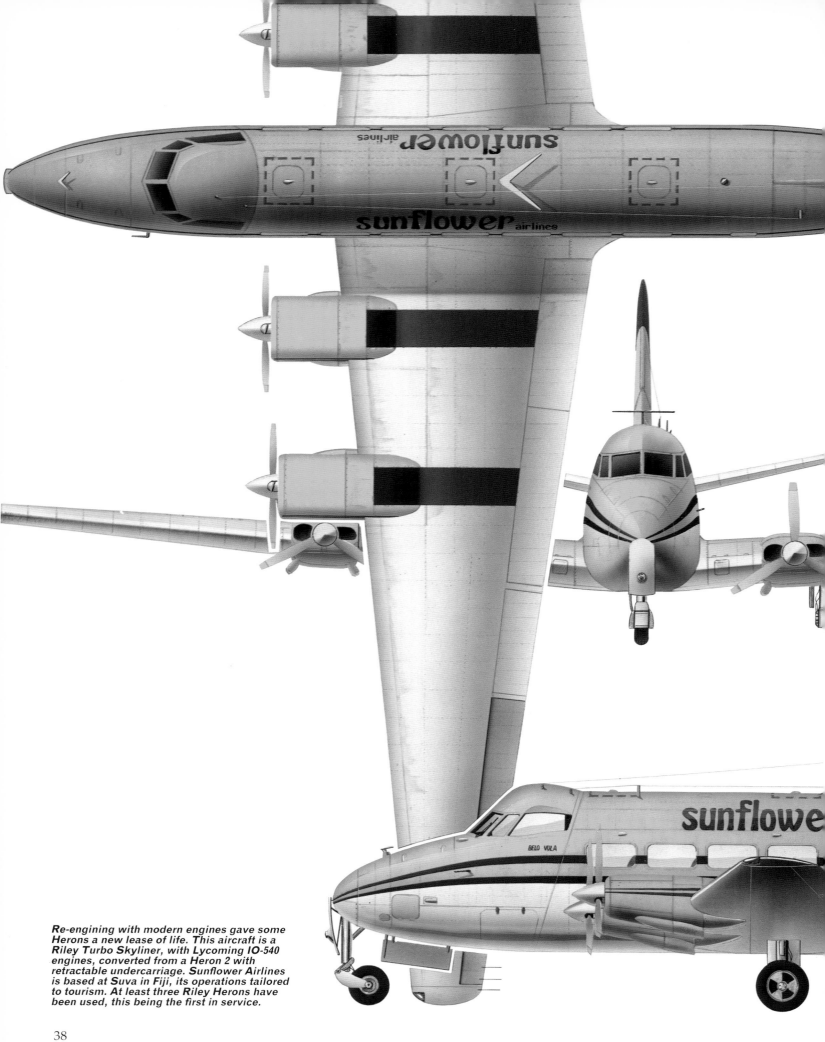

Re-engining with modern engines gave some Herons a new lease of life. This aircraft is a Riley Turbo Skyliner, with Lycoming IO-540 engines, converted from a Heron 2 with retractable undercarriage. Sunflower Airlines is based at Suva in Fiji, its operations tailored to tourism. At least three Riley Herons have been used, this being the first in service.

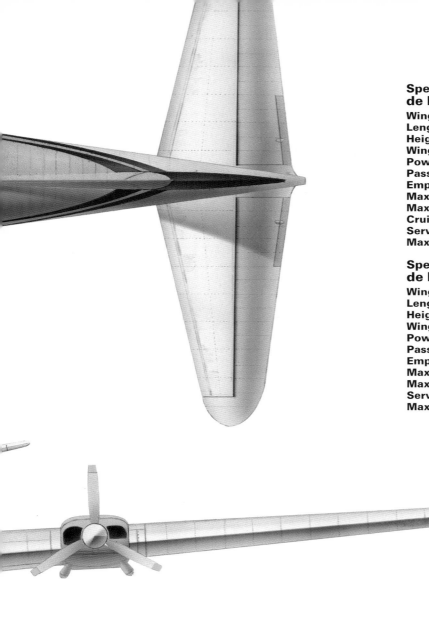

de Havilland D.H.104 Dove 1/D.H.114 Heron 2B

Specification
de Havilland D.H.104 Dove 1
Wingspan: 17.3 m (57 ft 0 in)
Length: 12.0 m (39 ft 4 in)
Height: 4.0 m (13 ft 4 in)
Wing area: 31 m² (335 sq ft)
Powerplant: two 246-kW (330-hp) D.H. Gipsy Queen 70-3
Passenger capacity: 8-11
Empty weight: 2562 kg (5,650 lb)
Maximum take-off weight: 3855 kg (8,500 lb)
Maximum speed: 323 km/h (201 mph)
Cruising speed: 265 km/h (165 mph)
Service ceiling: 6096 m (20,000 ft)
Maximum range: 1609 km (1,000 miles)

Specification
de Havilland D.H.114 Heron 2B
Wingspan: 21.8 m (71 ft 6 in)
Length: 14.8 m (48 ft 6 in)
Height: 4.7 m (15 ft 7 in)
Wing area: 46 m² (499 sq ft)
Powerplant: four 186-kW (250-hp) D.H. Gipsy Queen 30 Mark 2
Passenger capacity: 14-17
Empty weight: 3610 kg (7,960 lb)
Maximum take-off weight: 5896 kg (13,000 lb)
Maximum cruising speed: 257 km/h (160 mph)
Service ceiling: 5638 m (18,500 ft)
Maximum range: 1245 km (805 miles)

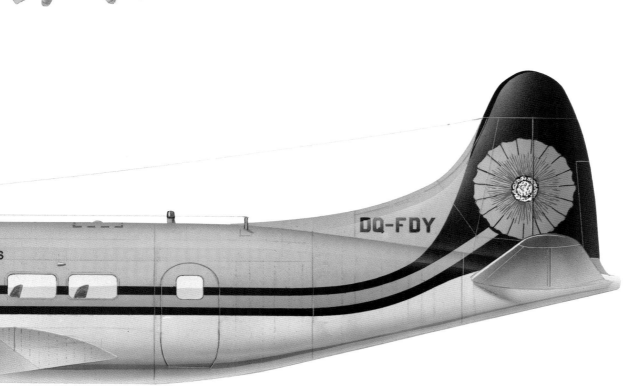

DQ-FDY

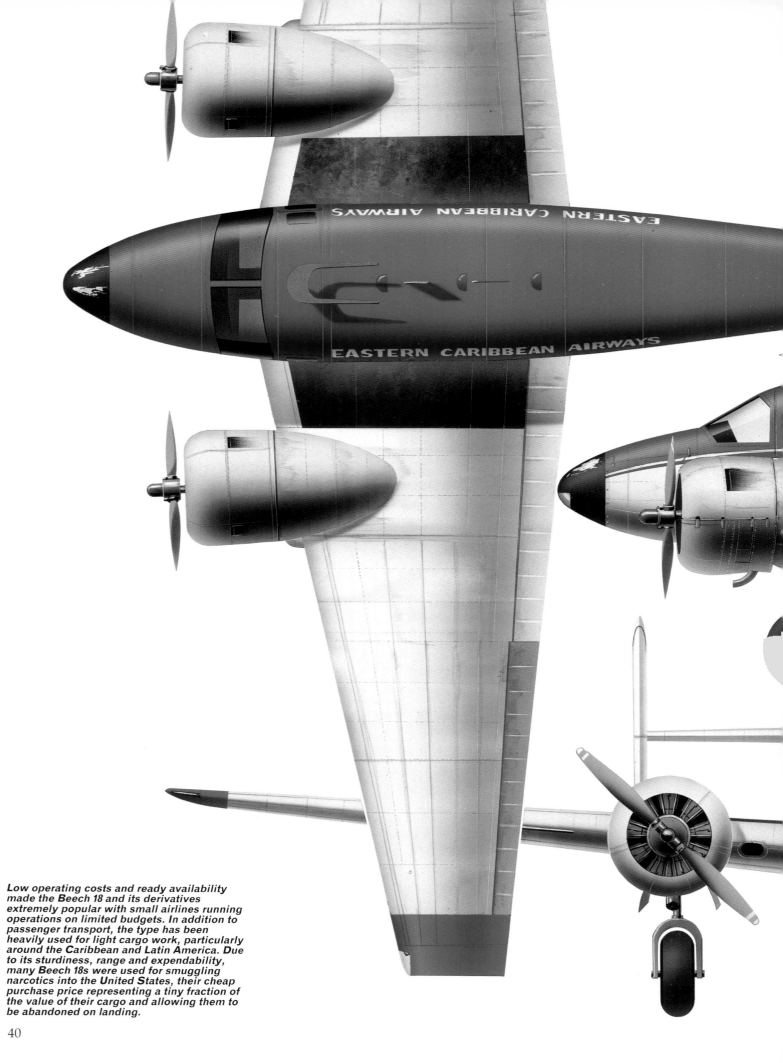

Low operating costs and ready availability made the **Beech 18** and its derivatives extremely popular with small airlines running operations on limited budgets. In addition to passenger transport, the type has been heavily used for light cargo work, particularly around the Caribbean and Latin America. Due to its sturdiness, range and expendability, many **Beech 18s** were used for smuggling narcotics into the United States, their cheap purchase price representing a tiny fraction of the value of their cargo and allowing them to be abandoned on landing.

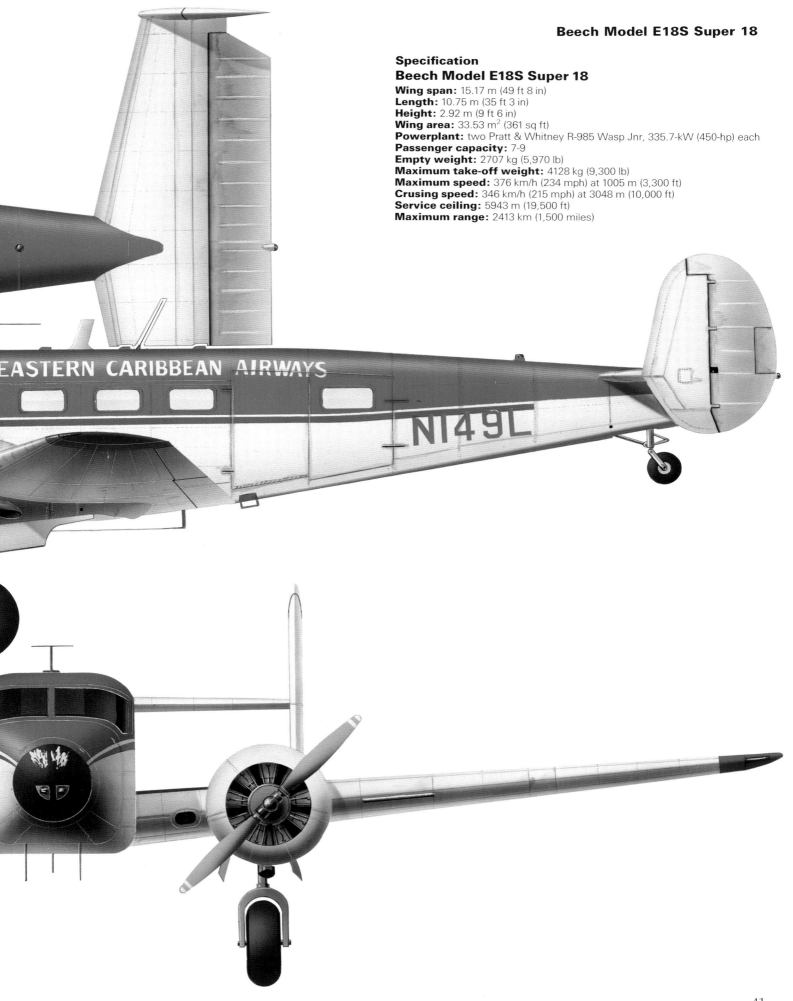

Specification
Beech Model E18S Super 18
Wing span: 15.17 m (49 ft 8 in)
Length: 10.75 m (35 ft 3 in)
Height: 2.92 m (9 ft 6 in)
Wing area: 33.53 m² (361 sq ft)
Powerplant: two Pratt & Whitney R-985 Wasp Jnr, 335.7-kW (450-hp) each
Passenger capacity: 7-9
Empty weight: 2707 kg (5,970 lb)
Maximum take-off weight: 4128 kg (9,300 lb)
Maximum speed: 376 km/h (234 mph) at 1005 m (3,300 ft)
Crusing speed: 346 km/h (215 mph) at 3048 m (10,000 ft)
Service ceiling: 5943 m (19,500 ft)
Maximum range: 2413 km (1,500 miles)

EASTERN CARIBBEAN AIRWAYS

N149L

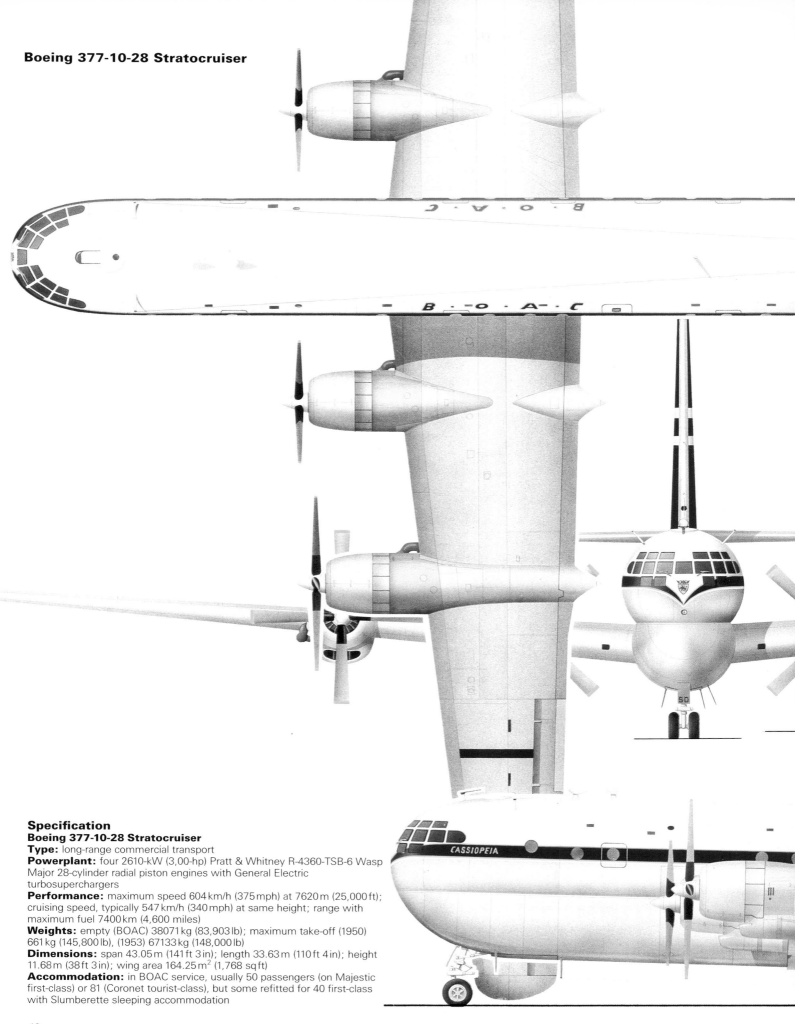

Boeing 377-10-28 Stratocruiser

Specification
Boeing 377-10-28 Stratocruiser
Type: long-range commercial transport
Powerplant: four 2610-kW (3,00-hp) Pratt & Whitney R-4360-TSB-6 Wasp Major 28-cylinder radial piston engines with General Electric turbosuperchargers
Performance: maximum speed 604 km/h (375 mph) at 7620 m (25,000 ft); cruising speed, typically 547 km/h (340 mph) at same height; range with maximum fuel 7400 km (4,600 miles)
Weights: empty (BOAC) 38071 kg (83,903 lb); maximum take-off (1950) 661 kg (145,800 lb), (1953) 67133 kg (148,000 lb)
Dimensions: span 43.05 m (141 ft 3 in); length 33.63 m (110 ft 4 in); height 11.68 m (38 ft 3 in); wing area 164.25 m² (1,768 sq ft)
Accommodation: in BOAC service, usually 50 passengers (on Majestic first-class) or 81 (Coronet tourist-class), but some refitted for 40 first-class with Slumberette sleeping accommodation

Boeing C-97 variants

XC-97 (Model 367-1): prototypes with 1641-kW (2,200-hp) Wright R-3350-23; total three
YC-97 (Model 367-5): 1734-kW (2,325-hp) R-3350-57A, bladder fuel cells, new electrical system, combustion heaters; total six
YC-97A (Model 367-4-6): 2237-kW (3,000-hp) Pratt & Whitney R-4360-35A Wasp Majors, tall folding fin, thermal de-icing; total three
C-97A (Model 367-4-19): increased fuel capacity, nose radar; total 50
KC-97A: three (49-2591, 2592, 2596) converted for tanker testing
YC-97B (Model 367-4-7): no rear ramp doors, passenger interior with passenger windows, one only (45-59596), became **C-97D**
C-97C (Model 367-4-29): strong cargo floor, extra equipment; total 14
MC-97C: conversions for Korean casevac service
VC-97D: conversions (3) as command posts, special communications and underwing fuel tanks
KC-97E (Model 367-4-29, as C): first production tanker, large above-floor tanks, refuelling boom; total 60
KC-97F (Model 367-76-29): 2834-kW (3,800-hp) P&W R-4360-59B engines; total 159
KC-97G (Model 367-76-66): tanker/transport with full cargo provision plus transfer fuel (including underwing tanks) and boom; total 592
C-97G: conversions (135) as pure transports with FR gear removed
EC-97G: conversions (3) for special electronic duties
HC-97G: conversions (29+) for interim search and rescue
KC-97H: conversion of KC-97F 51-332 for probe/drogue flight refuelling
YC-97J (Model 367-86-542): at first designated **YC-137**, then **YC-97H**, conversions (two, 52-2693, 2762) with 4250-kW (5,700-hp) T34-5A turboprop engines
C-97K: conversions (27) as SAC mission support transports with passenger interior (boom retained)
KC-97L: conversions (82) by Hayes Aircraft with underwing tanks replaced by J47-25A booster jet pods
Model 377-10-19: company prototype Stratocruiser, NX90700
Model 377-10-26: Pan Am, round windows, 61 day seats, 18 night berths to sleep 27 plus 25 seated; NC1023V/1024V
Model 377-10-28: SAS (taken over by BOAC), 55 day seats plus two upper-deck staterooms, 17 berths to sleep 26 plus 20 seats; G-ALSA/ALSD
Model 377-10-29: AOA, 60 day seats, 30 berths to sleep 45 plus 25 seated; NC90941/90948
Model 377-10-30: NWA (Northwest), square windows, 61 day seats, 16 berths to sleep 24 plus 29 seated; NC74601/74610
Model 377-10-32: BOAC, 60 main-deck seats plus 12 lower-deck lounges, 16 berths to sleep 24 plus 28 seats; G-AKGH/AKGM
Model 377-10-34: UAL (United), square windows, aft stateroom plus 55 day seats, 17 berths to sleep 26 plus 20 or 28 seats; NC31225/31231
B-377PG Pregnant Guppy: Pan Am aircraft rebuilt, R-4360-B6 engines, 6.02m (19ft 9in) upper lobe; N1024V
B-377SG Super Guppy: total rebuild, 7.62-m (25-ft) upper lobe, 5220-kW (7,000-hp) T34-7WA turboprops; N1038V
B-377MG Mini Guppy: longer fuselage and wing centre section, modestly enlarged swing-tail fuselage, cargo width 5.5m (18ft), R-4360-B6 engines; N1037V
Guppy-101 Commercial SG: 3669-kW (4,920-hp) Allison 501-D22C turboprops, crashed on early test
Guppy-201: definitive model for large airframe haulage, cabin length 33.99m (11ft 6in), pressurised, 110° swing nose, first aircraft N211AS, subsequent examples likewise registered as new: Airbus Industrie uses four aircraft subcontracted to Aéromaritime, registered from F-BPPA, the fourth entering service in August 1983

In the immediate post-war years, strong nationalist feelings in Britain resulted in an outcry when a fleet of Boeing Stratocruisers was purchased in 1948, whereas today it is no longer controversial for British Airways to be totally dependent on American aircraft. BOAC bought six Model 377-10-32s, built to the airline's specification, followed by four 377-10-28s built to SAS order but diverted to the British carrier. G-ALSD was the fourth ex-SAS machine. All 10 were named after Short S.23 'Empire' flying-boats. In 1954, following the grounding of the Comet I, BOAC bought seven more 'Strats': six 377-10-34s from United Airlines and a 377-10-26 from Pan Am. After Cathay (G-ALSA, the first Stratocruiser delivered to the airline) had crashed on Christmas Day 1954, this left a total fleet of 16.

M. Badrocke

Antonov An-2P/An-2R

Specification
Antonov An-2P/An-2R

Type: (P) 12-passenger transport; (R) agricultural sprayer/duster
Powerplant: one 745.7-kW (1,000-hp) PZL ASz-62IR (Soviet ASh-62IR) 9-cylinder radial piston engine
Performance: maximum speed at low level 258 km/h (160 mph); cruising speed 185 km/h (115 mph); minimum flying speed 90 km/h (56 mph); take-off run (paved runway) 150 m (492 ft); range with 500-kg (1,102-lb) payload, 900 km (560 miles)
Weights: empty (P) 3450 kg (7,605 lb); maximum 5500 kg (12,125 lb)
Dimensions: span 18.18 m (59 ft 7.75 in); length 14.24 m (46 ft 8.63 in); height 4.00 m (13 ft 2.48 in); wing area 71.6 m^2 (770 sq ft)
Accommodation: cockpit for pilot and engineer; main cabin (2P) with seats for up to 12 passengers with overhead racks for 160 kg (352 lb) baggage

Variants

SKh-1: two prototypes, the first with ASh-21 engine

Soviet Union
An-2F: see An-2NRK
An-2K: see An-2NRK
An-2L: first firefighting model; landplane with tank and dropped chemicals
An-2M: revised 1964 version built only by Antonov OKB
An-2NRK: night reconnaissance and artillery correction model; major redesign
An-2P: basic passenger version seating 14
An-2PP: seaplane water-bomber for forest firefighting
An-2S: ambulance version
An-2SKh: agricultural version
An-2T: multi-role utility transport/tug
An-2TD: parachute trainer
An-2TP: comfortable airliner version for 12 passengers
An-2V: seaplane version
An-2ZA: high-altitude atmospheric sampling laboratory
An-3: new turboprop version
An-4: original designation of An-2V
An-6: high-altitude utility transport for mountainous regions

Poland
An-2 Geofiz: geophysical survey model, developed for State Prospecting Company
An-2LW: seaplane version
An-2M: original designation of An-2LW
An-2P: post-1968 passenger model for 12 adults plus two children
An-2PK: five-seat executive version
An-2PF: photogrammetric and survey version
An-2PR: TV relay platform
An-2R: agricultural model with an epoxy-resin hopper for 1350 kg (2,976 lb) or 1400-litre (308-Imp gal) tank
An-2S: ambulance version
An-2T: utility version for 12 seats or 1500 kg (3,307 lb) of cargo
An-2TD: paratroop trainer with six seats on each side
An-2TP: convertible cargo/passenger with six tip-up seats each side

China
Y-5: basic Chinese designation, sub-variants unknown

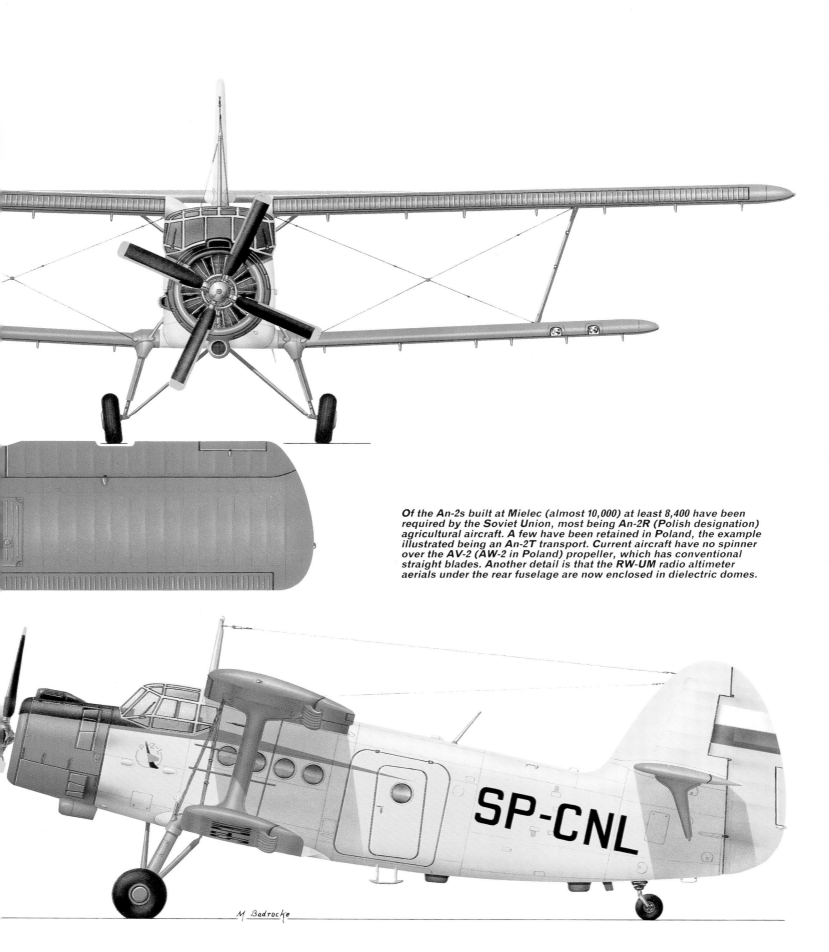

Of the An-2s built at Mielec (almost 10,000) at least 8,400 have been required by the Soviet Union, most being An-2R (Polish designation) agricultural aircraft. A few have been retained in Poland, the example illustrated being an An-2T transport. Current aircraft have no spinner over the AV-2 (AW-2 in Poland) propeller, which has conventional straight blades. Another detail is that the RW-UM radio altimeter aerials under the rear fuselage are now enclosed in dielectric domes.

SP-CNL

M Badrocke

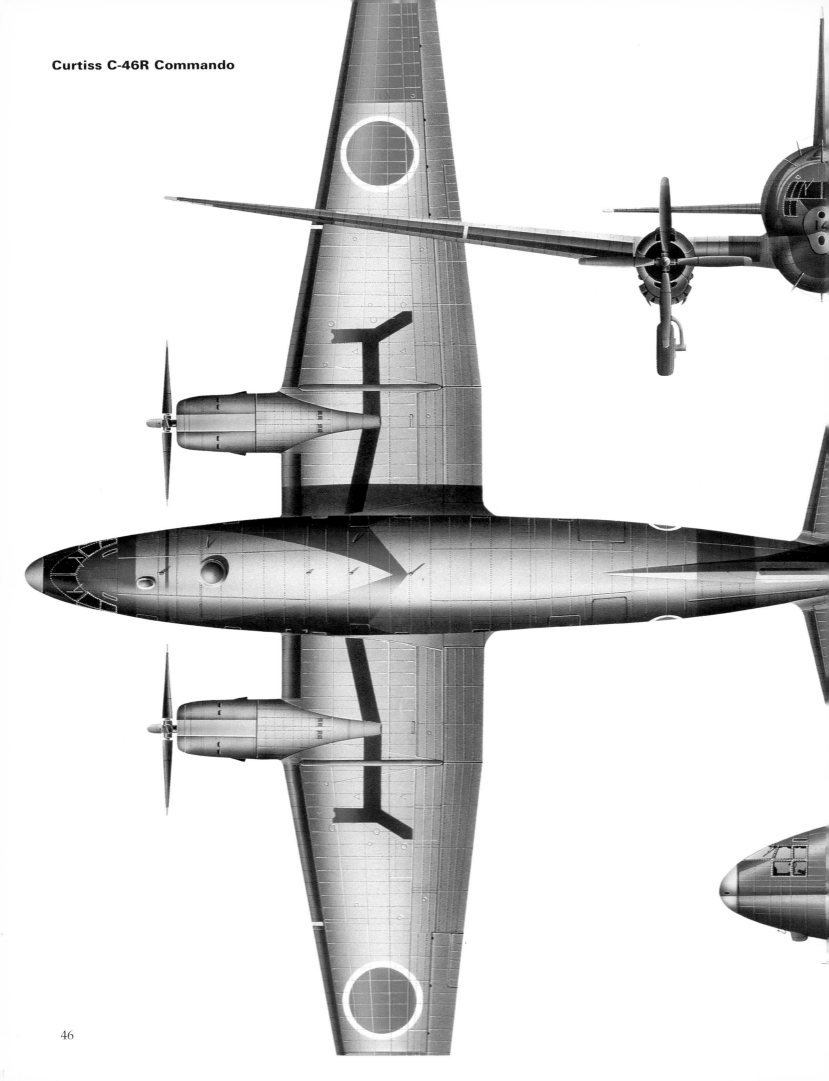

Curtiss C-46R Commando

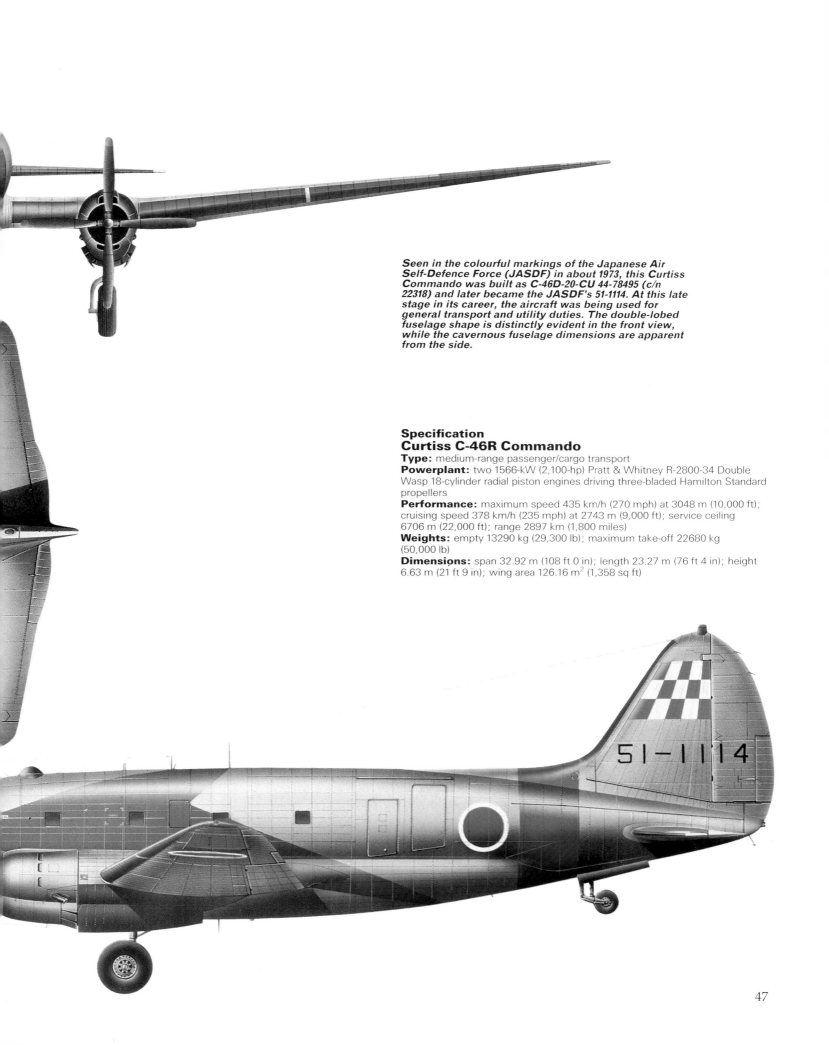

Seen in the colourful markings of the Japanese Air Self-Defence Force (JASDF) in about 1973, this Curtiss Commando was built as C-46D-20-CU 44-78495 (c/n 22318) and later became the JASDF's 51-1114. At this late stage in its career, the aircraft was being used for general transport and utility duties. The double-lobed fuselage shape is distinctly evident in the front view, while the cavernous fuselage dimensions are apparent from the side.

Specification
Curtiss C-46R Commando

Type: medium-range passenger/cargo transport

Powerplant: two 1566-kW (2,100-hp) Pratt & Whitney R-2800-34 Double Wasp 18-cylinder radial piston engines driving three-bladed Hamilton Standard propellers

Performance: maximum speed 435 km/h (270 mph) at 3048 m (10,000 ft); cruising speed 378 km/h (235 mph) at 2743 m (9,000 ft); service ceiling 6706 m (22,000 ft); range 2897 km (1,800 miles)

Weights: empty 13290 kg (29,300 lb); maximum take-off 22680 kg (50,000 lb)

Dimensions: span 32.92 m (108 ft 0 in); length 23.27 m (76 ft 4 in); height 6.63 m (21 ft 9 in); wing area 126.16 m² (1,358 sq ft)

de Havilland Canada Beaver

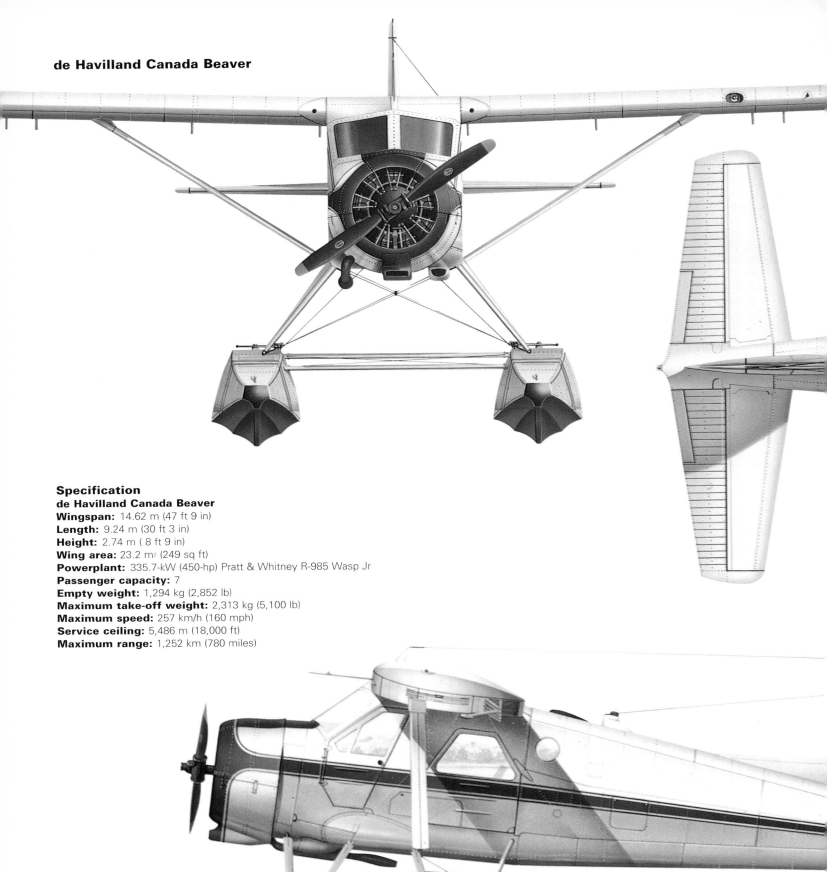

Specification
de Havilland Canada Beaver
Wingspan: 14.62 m (47 ft 9 in)
Length: 9.24 m (30 ft 3 in)
Height: 2.74 m (8 ft 9 in)
Wing area: 23.2 m² (249 sq ft)
Powerplant: 335.7-kW (450-hp) Pratt & Whitney R-985 Wasp Jr
Passenger capacity: 7
Empty weight: 1,294 kg (2,852 lb)
Maximum take-off weight: 2,313 kg (5,100 lb)
Maximum speed: 257 km/h (160 mph)
Service ceiling: 5,486 m (18,000 ft)
Maximum range: 1,252 km (780 miles)

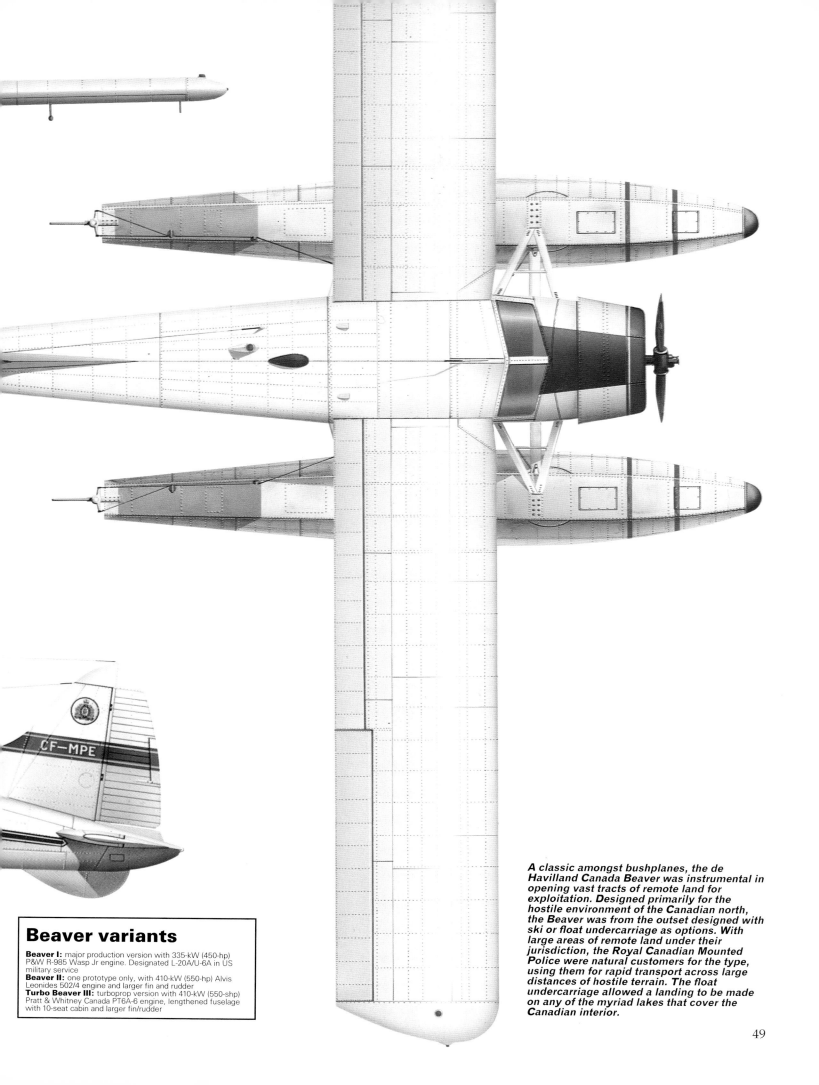

Beaver variants

Beaver I: major production version with 335-kW (450-hp) P&W R-985 Wasp Jr engine. Designated L-20A/U-6A in US military service
Beaver II: one prototype only, with 410-kW (550-hp) Alvis Leonides 502/4 engine and larger fin and rudder
Turbo Beaver III: turboprop version with 410-kW (550-shp) Pratt & Whitney Canada PT6A-6 engine, lengthened fuselage with 10-seat cabin and larger fin/rudder

A classic amongst bushplanes, the de Havilland Canada Beaver was instrumental in opening vast tracts of remote land for exploitation. Designed primarily for the hostile environment of the Canadian north, the Beaver was from the outset designed with ski or float undercarriage as options. With large areas of remote land under their jurisdiction, the Royal Canadian Mounted Police were natural customers for the type, using them for rapid transport across large distances of hostile terrain. The float undercarriage allowed a landing to be made on any of the myriad lakes that cover the Canadian interior.

Boeing 307 Stratoliner

Specification
Boeing 307 Stratoliner
Wingspan: 32.7 m (107 ft 3 in)
Length: 22.7 m (74 ft 4 in)
Height: 6.3 m (20 ft 9 in)
Wing area: 138 m² (1,486 sq ft)
Powerplant: four 671.4-kW (900-hp) Wright GR-1820 Cyclone engines
Passenger capacity: 33
Empty weight: 13750 kg (30,310 lb)
Maximum take-off weight: 19050 kg (42,000 lb)
Maximum speed: 396 km/h (246 mph)
Cruising speed: 355 km/h (220 mph)
Service ceiling: 7985 m (26,200 ft)
Maximum range: 3846 km (2,390 miles)

Although Pan American was the launch customer for the Model 307, it was TWA which had the largest fleet (five) and was the best-known operator. This aircraft was the machine which undertook a sales trip for the impending introduction of the Model 307B (as TWA's aircraft were designated), and received the spurious serial NX1940 to mark the event. Its real identity was NX19906. Internally the Stratoliner featured four cabins down the starboard side, partitioned by wood panels across the cabin, and separated from the aisle by a curtain. Down the port side of the aircraft were nine luxurious chairs. A lavatory was at the front, while the rear of the cabin had a galley and ladies' room. A crew of five flew the aircraft, consisting of two pilots facing forward, wireless operator (port) and flight engineer (starboard) facing outwards behind them, and a navigator facing outwards to starboard in a separate cabin behind the engineer.

NX1940

401

STRATOLINER

BOEING

TWA

Douglas C-54G Skymaster

Specification
Douglas C-54G Skymaster

Type: long-range transport

Powerplant: four 1081-kW (1,450-shp) Pratt & Whitney R-2000-9 Twin Wasp radial piston engines

Performance: maximum speed 451 km/h (280 mph) at 4265 m (14,000 ft); cruising speed 349 km/h (217 mph) at 2590 m (8,500 ft); service ceiling 6800 m (22,300 ft); range 4023 km (2,500 miles) with 5189-kg (11,440-lb) payload

Weights: empty 19641 kg (43,300 lb); maximum take-off 33113 kg (73,000 lb)

Dimensions: span 35.81 m (117 ft 6 in); length 28.60 m (93 ft 10 in); height 8.38 m (27 ft 6 in); wing area 135.63 m² (1,460 sq ft)

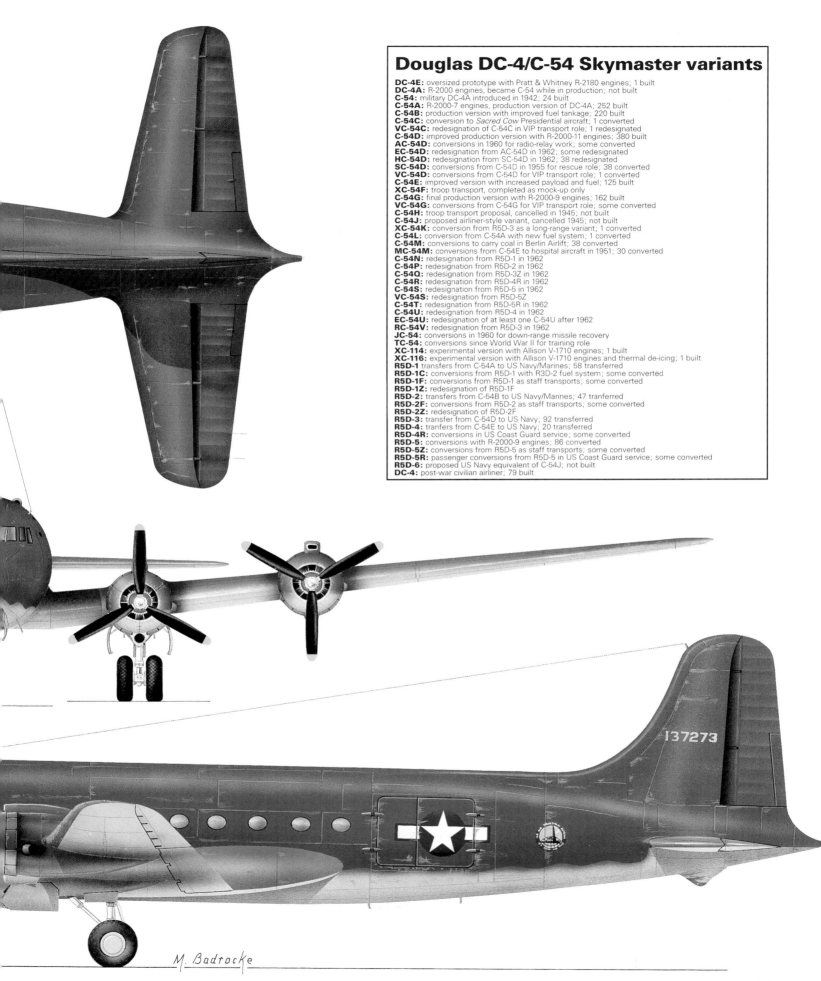

Douglas DC-4/C-54 Skymaster variants

DC-4E: oversized prototype with Pratt & Whitney R-2180 engines; 1 built
DC-4A: R-2000 engines, became C-54 while in production; not built
C-54: military DC-4A introduced in 1942; 24 built
C-54A: R-2000-7 engines, production version of DC-4A; 252 built
C-54B: production version with improved fuel tankage; 220 built
C-54C: conversion to *Sacred Cow* Presidential aircraft; 1 converted
VC-54C: redesignation of C-54C in VIP transport role; 1 redesignated
C-54D: improved production version with R-2000-11 engines; 380 built
AC-54D: conversions in 1960 for radio-relay work; some converted
EC-54D: redesignation from AC-54D in 1962; some redesignated
HC-54D: redesignation from SC-54D in 1962; 38 redesignated
SC-54D: conversions from C-54D in 1955 for rescue role; 38 converted
VC-54D: conversions from C-54D for VIP transport role; 1 converted
C-54E: improved version with increased payload and fuel; 125 built
XC-54F: troop transport, completed as mock-up only
C-54G: final production version with R-2000-9 engines; 162 built
VC-54G: conversions from C-54G for VIP transport role; some converted
C-54H: troop transport proposal, cancelled in 1945; not built
C-54J: proposed airliner-style variant, cancelled 1945; not built
XC-54K: conversion from R5D-3 as a long-range variant; 1 converted
C-54L: conversion from C-54A with new fuel system; 1 converted
C-54M: conversions to carry coal in Berlin Airlift; 38 converted
MC-54M: conversions from C-54E to hospital aircraft in 1951; 30 converted
C-54N: redesignation from R5D-1 in 1962
C-54P: redesignation from R5D-2 in 1962
C-54Q: redesignation from R5D-3Z in 1962
C-54R: redesignation from R5D-4R in 1962
C-54S: redesignation from R5D-5 in 1962
VC-54S: redesignation from R5D-5Z
C-54T: redesignation from R5D-5R in 1962
C-54U: redesignation from R5D-4 in 1962
EC-54U: redesignation of at least one C-54U after 1962
RC-54V: redesignation from R5D-3 in 1962
JC-54: conversions in 1960 for down-range missile recovery
TC-54: conversions since World War II for training role
XC-114: experimental version with Allison V-1710 engines; 1 built
XC-116: experimental version with Allison V-1710 engines and thermal de-icing; 1 built
R5D-1: transfers from C-54A to US Navy/Marines; 58 transferred
R5D-1C: conversions from R5D-1 with R3D-2 fuel system; some converted
R5D-1F: conversions from R5D-1 as staff transports; some converted
R5D-1Z: redesignation of R5D-1F
R5D-2: transfers from C-54B to US Navy/Marines; 47 tranferred
R5D-2F: conversions from R5D-2 as staff transports; some converted
R5D-2Z: redesignation of R5D-2F
R5D-3: transfer from C-54D to US Navy; 92 transferred
R5D-4: tranfers from C-54E to US Navy; 20 transferred
R5D-4R: conversions in US Coast Guard service; some converted
R5D-5: conversions with R-2000-9 engines; 86 converted
R5D-5Z: conversions from R5D-5 as staff transports; some converted
R5D-5R: passenger conversions from R5D-5 in US Coast Guard service; some converted
R5D-6: proposed US Navy equivalent of C-54J; not built
DC-4: post-war civilian airliner; 79 built

M. Badrocke

137273

A.W.650 Argosy 100/222/A.W.660 Argosy C.Mk 1

Specification
A.W.650 Argosy 100
Powerplant: four Rolls-Royce RDa.7/2 526 turboprops, 1567 kW (2,100 shp) each
Wing span: 35.05 m (115 ft)
Length: 26.44 m (86 ft 9 in)
Height: 8.23 m (27 ft)
Wing area: 135.45 m² (1,458 sq ft)
Empty weight: 22000 kg (48,500 lb)
Maximum take-off weight: 39917 kg (88,000 lb)
Payload: 12700 kg (28,000 lb)
Cruising speed: 476 km/h (296 mph)
Maximum range: 4345 km (2,700 miles)

Specification
A.W.650 Argosy 222
Powerplant: four Rolls-Royce Dart 532/l turboprops, 1664 kW (2,230 shp) each
Wing span: 35.05 m (115 ft)
Length: 26.44 m (86 ft 9 in)
Height: 8.91 m (29 ft 3 in)
Wing area: 135.45 m² (1,458 sq ft)
Empty weight: 22136 kg (48,800 lb)
Maximum take-off weight: 42185 kg (93,000 lb)
Payload: 14061 kg (31,000 lb)
Cruising speed: 462 km/h (287 mph)
Range: maximum 3510 km (2180 miles), with maximum payload 1667 km (1035 miles)

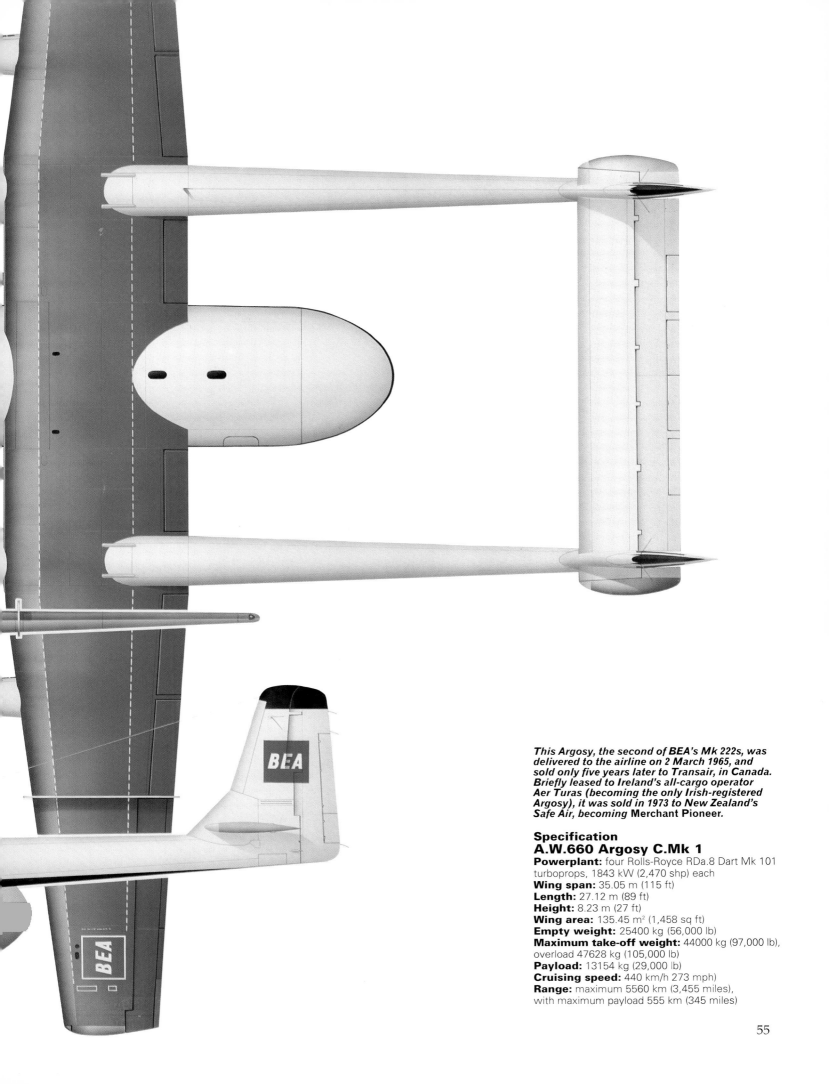

This Argosy, the second of BEA's Mk 222s, was delivered to the airline on 2 March 1965, and sold only five years later to Transair, in Canada. Briefly leased to Ireland's all-cargo operator Aer Turas (becoming the only Irish-registered Argosy), it was sold in 1973 to New Zealand's Safe Air, becoming Merchant Pioneer.

Specification
A.W.660 Argosy C.Mk 1
Powerplant: four Rolls-Royce RDa.8 Dart Mk 101 turboprops, 1843 kW (2,470 shp) each
Wing span: 35.05 m (115 ft)
Length: 27.12 m (89 ft)
Height: 8.23 m (27 ft)
Wing area: 135.45 m² (1,458 sq ft)
Empty weight: 25400 kg (56,000 lb)
Maximum take-off weight: 44000 kg (97,000 lb), overload 47628 kg (105,000 lb)
Payload: 13154 kg (29,000 lb)
Cruising speed: 440 km/h 273 mph)
Range: maximum 5560 km (3,455 miles), with maximum payload 555 km (345 miles)

Vickers Viscount V.708

F-BGNK was the first Viscount to be built and the first to be exported, flying as a V.708 on 11 March 1953 and being delivered to Air France on 18 May. It was one of the very few Viscounts to crash fatally; during a crew training flight on 12 December 1956 it dived into the ground near Paris, killing the five Air France crew. The flight-deck windows were common to all early aircraft (though not quite the same as on the V.630 and 663); TCA asked for larger vertical windows with pull-in direct vision, and this became standard. Under the rear fuselage is the cabin air system ram inlet.

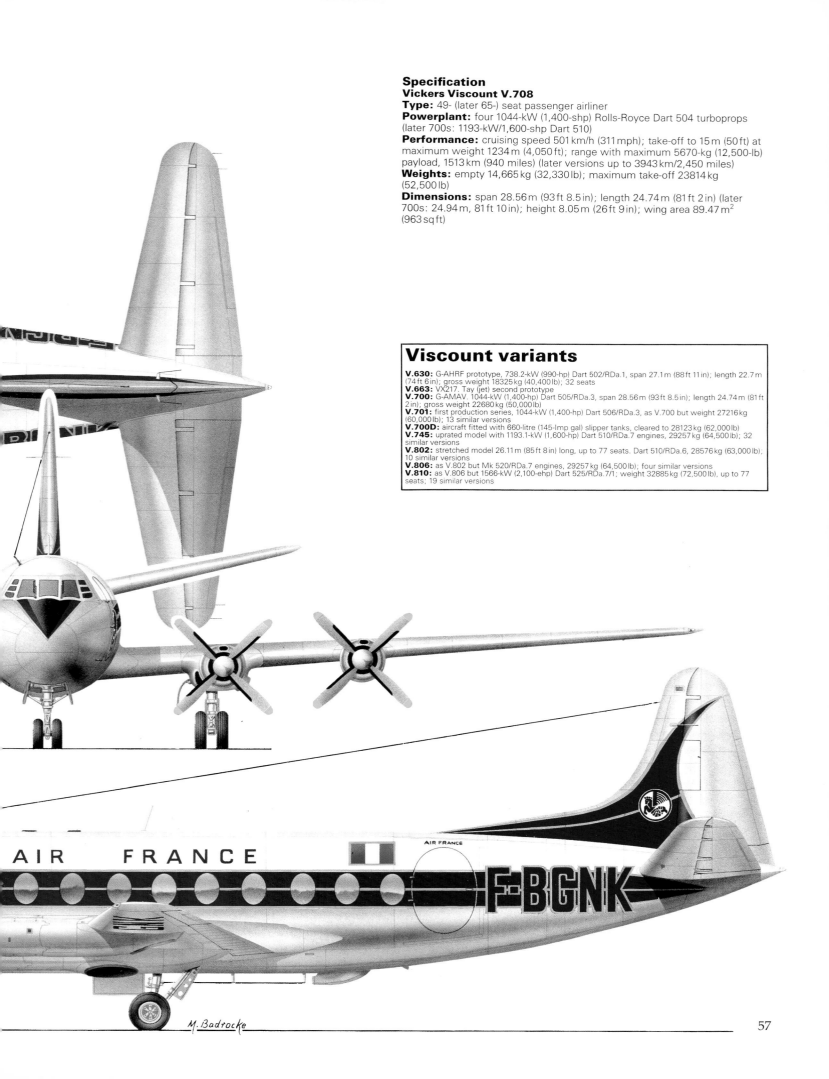

Specification
Vickers Viscount V.708
Type: 49- (later 65-) seat passenger airliner
Powerplant: four 1044-kW (1,400-shp) Rolls-Royce Dart 504 turboprops (later 700s: 1193-kW/1,600-shp Dart 510)
Performance: cruising speed 501 km/h (311 mph); take-off to 15 m (50 ft) at maximum weight 1234 m (4,050 ft); range with maximum 5670-kg (12,500-lb) payload, 1513 km (940 miles) (later versions up to 3943 km/2,450 miles)
Weights: empty 14,665 kg (32,330 lb); maximum take-off 23814 kg (52,500 lb)
Dimensions: span 28.56 m (93 ft 8.5 in); length 24.74 m (81 ft 2 in) (later 700s: 24.94 m, 81 ft 10 in); height 8.05 m (26 ft 9 in); wing area 89.47 m² (963 sq ft)

Viscount variants

V.630: G-AHRF prototype, 738.2-kW (990-hp) Dart 502/RDa.1, span 27.1 m (88 ft 11 in); length 22.7 m (74 ft 6 in); gross weight 18325 kg (40,400 lb); 32 seats
V.663: VX217. Tay (jet) second prototype
V.700: G-AMAV. 1044-kW (1,400-hp) Dart 505/RDa.3, span 28.56 m (93 ft 8.5 in); length 24.74 m (81 ft 2 in); gross weight 22680 kg (50,000 lb)
V.701: first production series, 1044-kW (1,400-hp) Dart 506/RDa.3, as V.700 but weight 27216 kg (60,000 lb); 13 similar versions
V.700D: aircraft fitted with 660-litre (145-Imp gal) slipper tanks, cleared to 28123 kg (62,000 lb)
V.745: uprated model with 1193.1-kW (1,600-hp) Dart 510/RDa.7 engines, 29257 kg (64,500 lb); 32 similar versions
V.802: stretched model 26.11 m (85 ft 8 in) long, up to 77 seats. Dart 510/RDa.6, 28576 kg (63,000 lb); 10 similar versions
V.806: as V.802 but Mk 520/RDa.7 engines, 29257 kg (64,500 lb); four similar versions
V.810: as V.806 but 1566-kW (2,100-ehp) Dart 525/RDa.7/1; weight 32885 kg (72,500 lb), up to 77 seats; 19 similar versions

AIR FRANCE

AIR FRANCE

F-BGNK

M. Badrocke

Tupolev Tu-104B

With the introduction of the Tu-104 on Aeroflot's Moscow-Irkutsk route on 15 September 1956, the Soviet Union became the second nation to provide scheduled passenger services utilising turbojet-powered aircraft. Advanced features of the machine included slotted trailing-edge flaps, boundary layer fences and an anti-skid braking system on the main landing gear units. One novel feature was a double braking parachute pack. Successive developments over the years increased passenger capacity by more than 100 per cent in addition to overall performance improvements, and though the design has only seen service with two operators, its place in airline history is assured as one of the pioneer designs.

Tupolev Tu-104 variants

Tu-88: bomber prototype powered by Mikulin RD-3 (AM-3) flown in 1952. Service designation **Tu-16**
Tu-104: airliner derivative of Tu-88 with new, enlarged fuselage and fuselage-mounted tailplane. Similar wing except for new wide centre section. Engine intakes moved outboard
Tu-104A: increased weight version with uprated AM-3M engines. Accommodation increased to 70
Tu-104B: AM-3M powered version with lengthened fuselage and standard accommodation of 100, later increased to 115
Tu-104D: Tu-104As refurnished to accommodate 85 passengers
Tu-104E: early Tu-104B modified for record-breaking purposes
Tu-104G: two Tu-16 bombers demilitarised for early crew training prior to Tu-104 services
Tu-104V: Tu-104A aircraft refurnished to seat 100 passengers
Tu-110: development similar to Tu-104B but powered by four Lyul'ka AL-5 turbojets

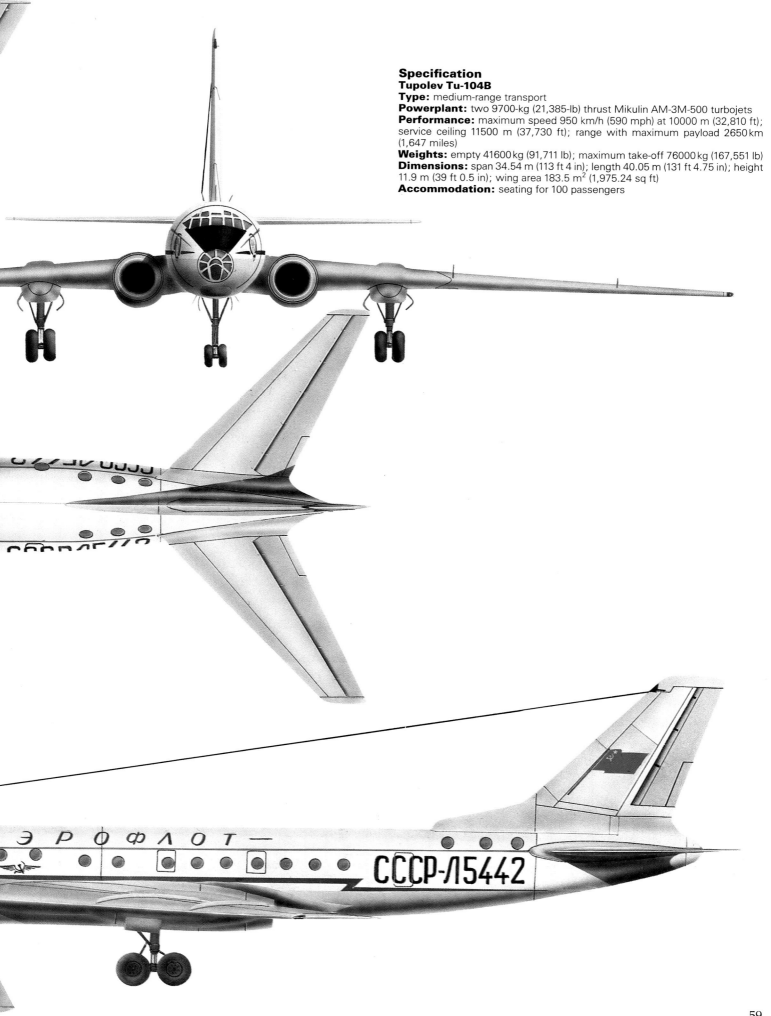

Specification
Tupolev Tu-104B
Type: medium-range transport
Powerplant: two 9700-kg (21,385-lb) thrust Mikulin AM-3M-500 turbojets
Performance: maximum speed 950 km/h (590 mph) at 10000 m (32,810 ft); service ceiling 11500 m (37,730 ft); range with maximum payload 2650 km (1,647 miles)
Weights: empty 41600 kg (91,711 lb); maximum take-off 76000 kg (167,551 lb)
Dimensions: span 34.54 m (113 ft 4 in); length 40.05 m (131 ft 4.75 in); height 11.9 m (39 ft 0.5 in); wing area 183.5 m² (1,975.24 sq ft)
Accommodation: seating for 100 passengers

de Havilland Canada DHC-3 Otter/Vardax Vazar Dash 3

Among the more colourful Otters was this aircraft operated by Wardair, which began as a local carrier but which rose to be a major transatlantic operator. During the winter months, Canadian Otters donned skis to continue services to remote settlements, while in summer floats were more appropriate for landing on the many lakes that dot the Canadian interior. The fuselage side door allowed the admission of sizeable cargo, and the Otters were regularly used to transport vital machinery.

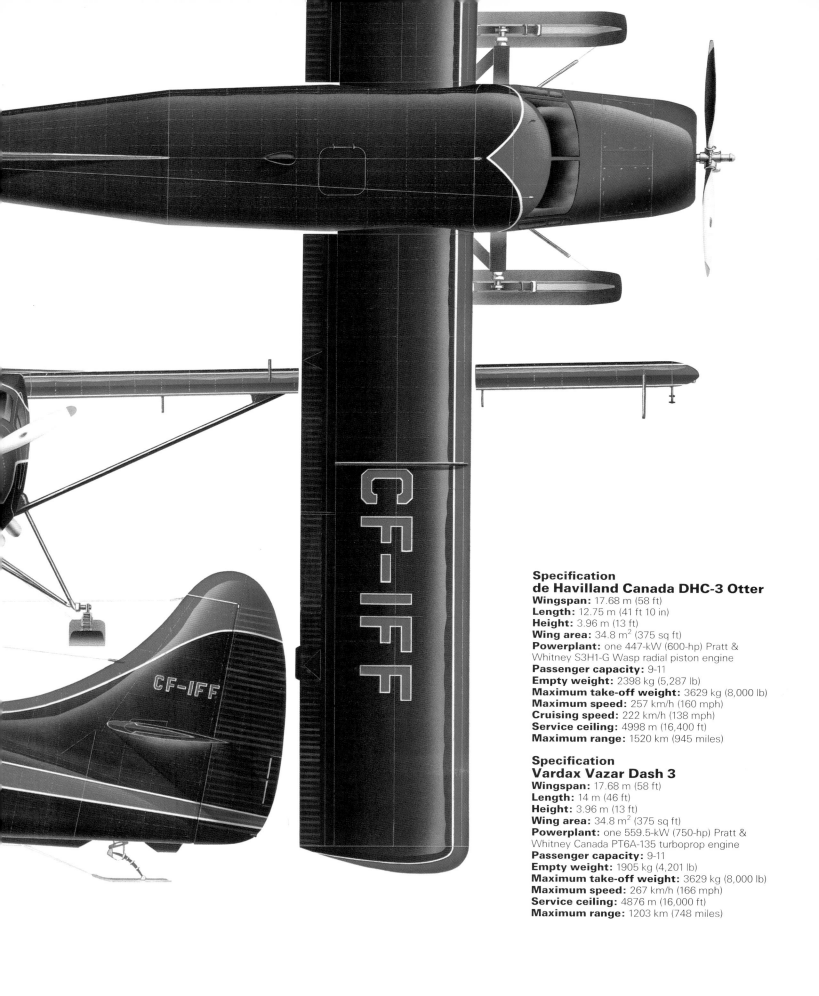

Specification
de Havilland Canada DHC-3 Otter
Wingspan: 17.68 m (58 ft)
Length: 12.75 m (41 ft 10 in)
Height: 3.96 m (13 ft)
Wing area: 34.8 m² (375 sq ft)
Powerplant: one 447-kW (600-hp) Pratt &
Whitney S3H1-G Wasp radial piston engine
Passenger capacity: 9-11
Empty weight: 2398 kg (5,287 lb)
Maximum take-off weight: 3629 kg (8,000 lb)
Maximum speed: 257 km/h (160 mph)
Cruising speed: 222 km/h (138 mph)
Service ceiling: 4998 m (16,400 ft)
Maximum range: 1520 km (945 miles)

Specification
Vardax Vazar Dash 3
Wingspan: 17.68 m (58 ft)
Length: 14 m (46 ft)
Height: 3.96 m (13 ft)
Wing area: 34.8 m² (375 sq ft)
Powerplant: one 559.5-kW (750-hp) Pratt &
Whitney Canada PT6A-135 turboprop engine
Passenger capacity: 9-11
Empty weight: 1905 kg (4,201 lb)
Maximum take-off weight: 3629 kg (8,000 lb)
Maximum speed: 267 km/h (166 mph)
Service ceiling: 4876 m (16,000 ft)
Maximum range: 1203 km (748 miles)

Vickers Viking 1B

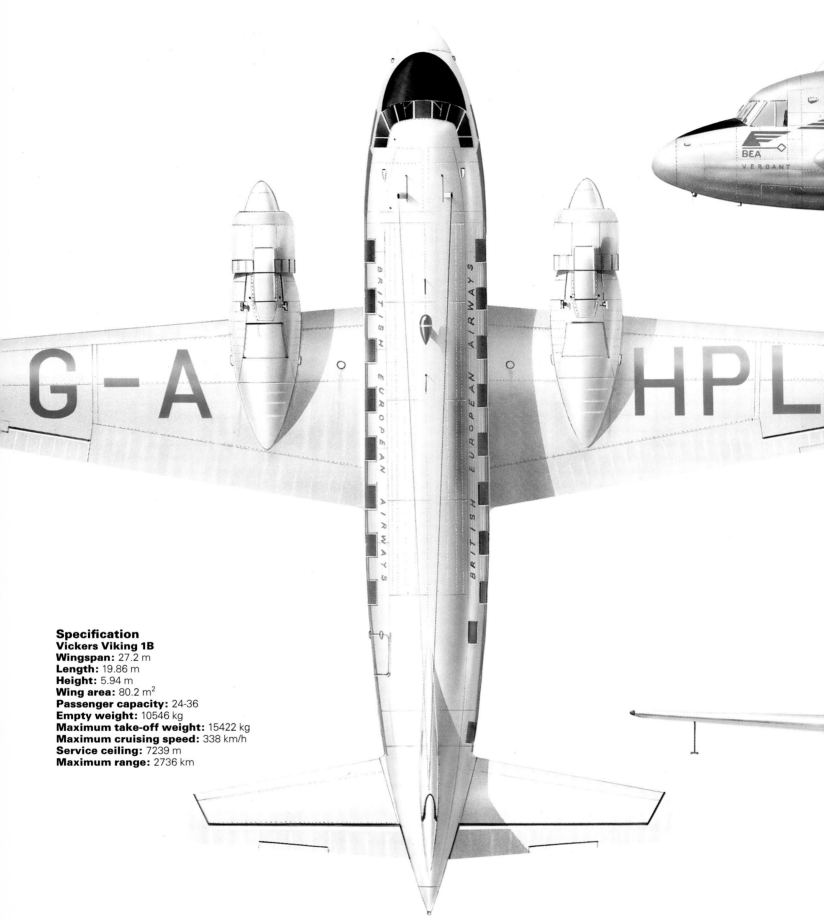

Specification
Vickers Viking 1B
Wingspan: 27.2 m
Length: 19.86 m
Height: 5.94 m
Wing area: 80.2 m²
Passenger capacity: 24-36
Empty weight: 10546 kg
Maximum take-off weight: 15422 kg
Maximum cruising speed: 338 km/h
Service ceiling: 7239 m
Maximum range: 2736 km

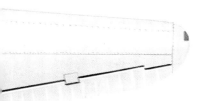

Despite achieving some notable export sales, the Viking is best-known in British European Airways service. At one time or another, the airline flew 76 of the 166 aircraft built, and these saw a gradual evolution of the airline's colour scheme. Technically the Viking was an advanced aircraft for its day which contributed to its longevity in service. The first few aircraft were completed with geodetic fabric-covered wings like the Wellington bomber, but these never saw operational service with BEA. All the later machines had stressed-skin metal wings, although flight surfaces remained fabric-covered.

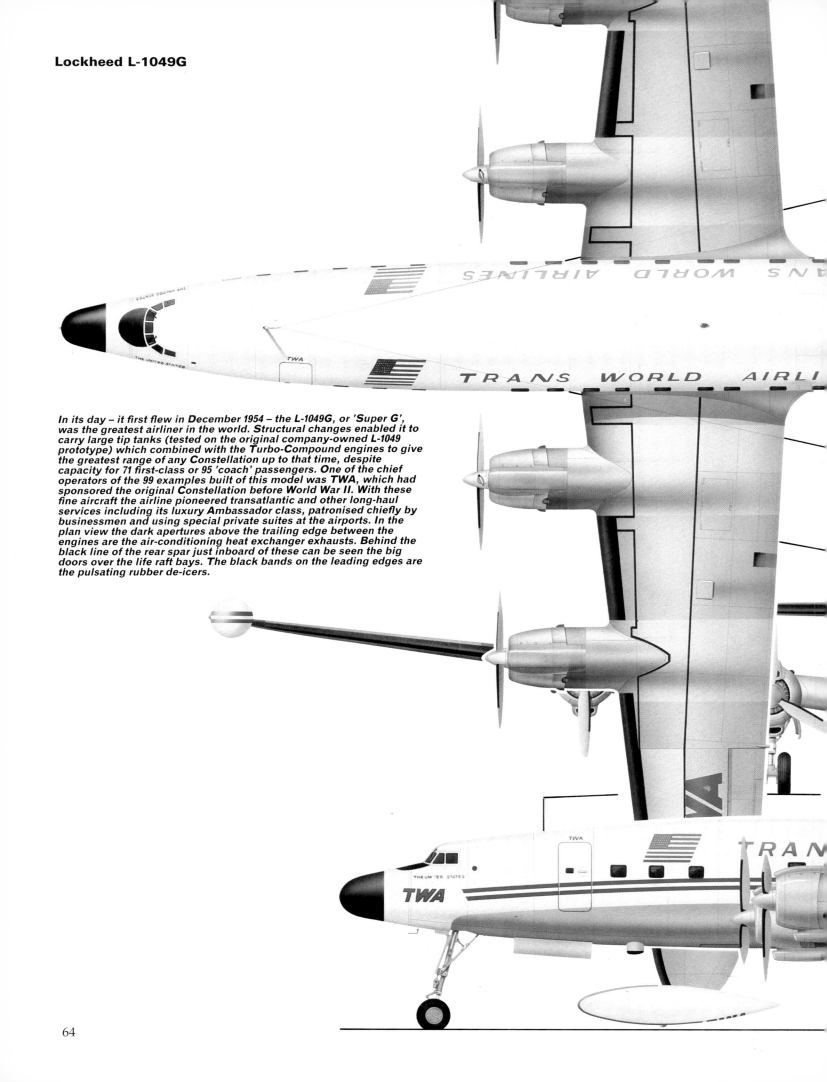

Lockheed L-1049G

TRANS WORLD AIRLINES

TRANS WORLD AIRLI

In its day – it first flew in December 1954 – the L-1049G, or 'Super G', was the greatest airliner in the world. Structural changes enabled it to carry large tip tanks (tested on the original company-owned L-1049 prototype) which combined with the Turbo-Compound engines to give the greatest range of any Constellation up to that time, despite capacity for 71 first-class or 95 'coach' passengers. One of the chief operators of the 99 examples built of this model was TWA, which had sponsored the original Constellation before World War II. With these fine aircraft the airline pioneered transatlantic and other long-haul services including its luxury Ambassador class, patronised chiefly by businessmen and using special private suites at the airports. In the plan view the dark apertures above the trailing edge between the engines are the air-conditioning heat exchanger exhausts. Behind the black line of the rear spar just inboard of these can be seen the big doors over the life raft bays. The black bands on the leading edges are the pulsating rubber de-icers.

TWA

TRAN

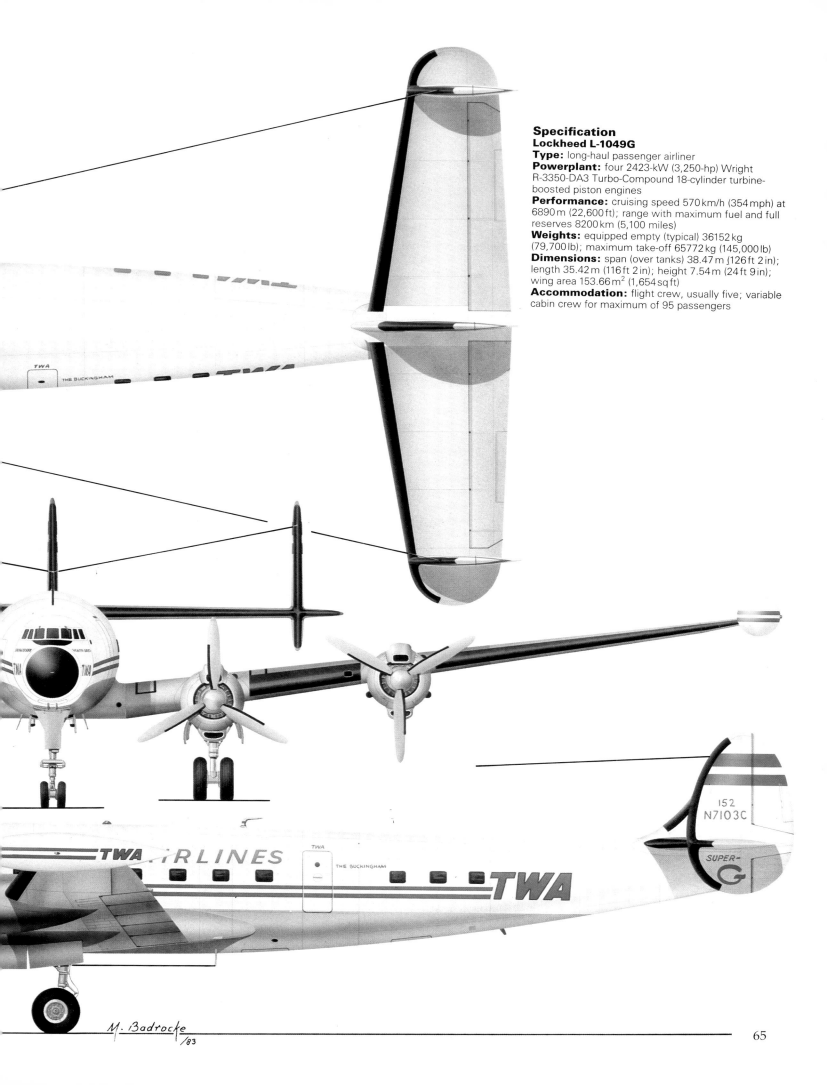

Specification
Lockheed L-1049G

Type: long-haul passenger airliner

Powerplant: four 2423-kW (3,250-hp) Wright R-3350-DA3 Turbo-Compound 18-cylinder turbine-boosted piston engines

Performance: cruising speed 570 km/h (354 mph) at 6890 m (22,600 ft); range with maximum fuel and full reserves 8200 km (5,100 miles)

Weights: equipped empty (typical) 36152 kg (79,700 lb); maximum take-off 65772 kg (145,000 lb)

Dimensions: span (over tanks) 38.47 m (126 ft 2 in); length 35.42 m (116 ft 2 in); height 7.54 m (24 ft 9 in); wing area 153.66 m² (1,654 sq ft)

Accommodation: flight crew, usually five; variable cabin crew for maximum of 95 passengers

M. Badrocke
/83

Lockheed L-188A Electra

Specification
Lockheed L-188A Electra
Wingspan: 30 m (99 ft 0 in)
Length: 32.14 m (104 ft 5½ in)
Height: 10.25 m (32 ft 9 in)
Wing area: 120.8 m² (1,300 sq ft)
Passenger capacity: 66-98
Empty weight: 26037 kg (57,400 lb)
Payload: 10353 kg (22,825 lb)
Maximum take-off weight: 51257 kg
(113,000 lb)
Economic cruising speed: 600 km/h
(373 mph)
Maximum cruising speed: 652 km/h
(405 mph)
Maximum speed: 721 km/h (448 mph)
Initial rate of climb: 600 m (1,970 ft/min)
Service ceiling: 8656 m (28,400 ft)
Maximum range: 4458 km (2,770 miles)
Range with maximum payload: 3540 km
(2,200 miles)

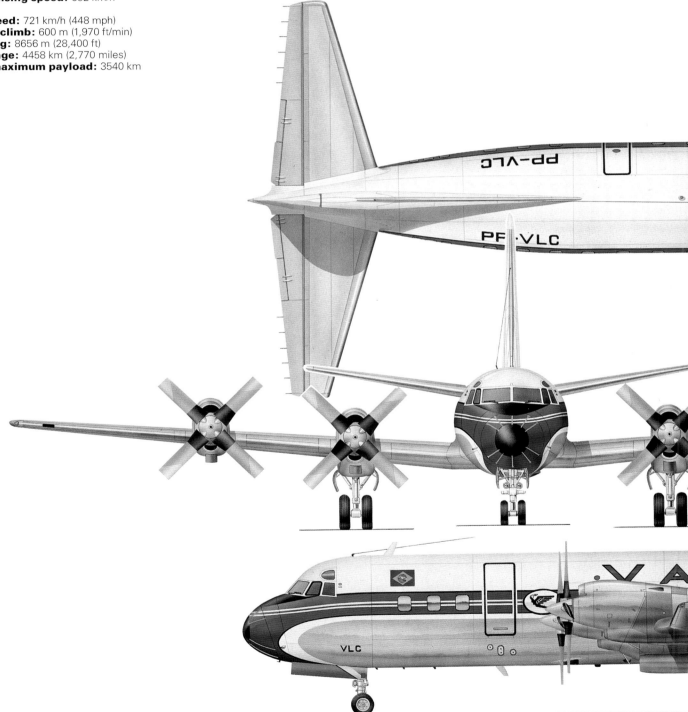

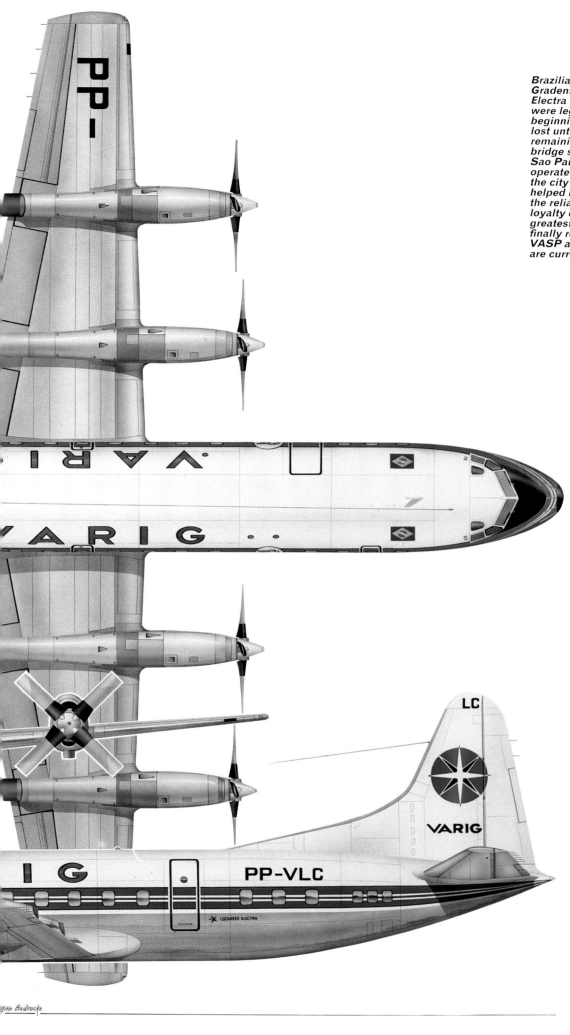

Brazilian airline **VARIG** (Viaço Aérea Rio-Gradense) was perhaps the most faithful Electra operator ever and their L-188 services were legend. Fifteen aircraft were delivered beginning in the early 1960s and only one was lost until their retirement in 1991. The remaining aircraft operated the daily air-bridge shuttle between Rio de Janeiro and Sao Paulo. The airport from which they were operated in Rio, Santos Dumont, was close to the city centre and closed to jet traffic. This helped in the Electra's longevity, but it was the reliability of its Allison engines and the loyalty of the passengers that were their greatest allies. The 90-seat propliners were finally replaced by a mixture of **VARIG**, **VASP** and TransBrasil Boeing 737-300s. All are currently in storage and awaiting a buyer.

Convair 240/440/580/640

Specification
Convair 240
Wingspan: 28 m (91 ft 9 in)
Length: 22.7 m (74 ft 8 in)
Height: 8.2 m (26 ft 11 in)
Wing area: 76 m² (817 sq ft)
Passenger capacity: 40
Empty weight: 13400 kg (29,500 lb)
Payload: 4400 kg (9,600 lb)
Max take-off weight: 19300 kg (42,500 lb)
Cruising speed: 450 km/h (280 mph)
Maximum speed: 506 km/h (315 mph)
Service ceiling: 6100 m (20,000 ft)
Maximum range: 1930 km (1,200 miles)

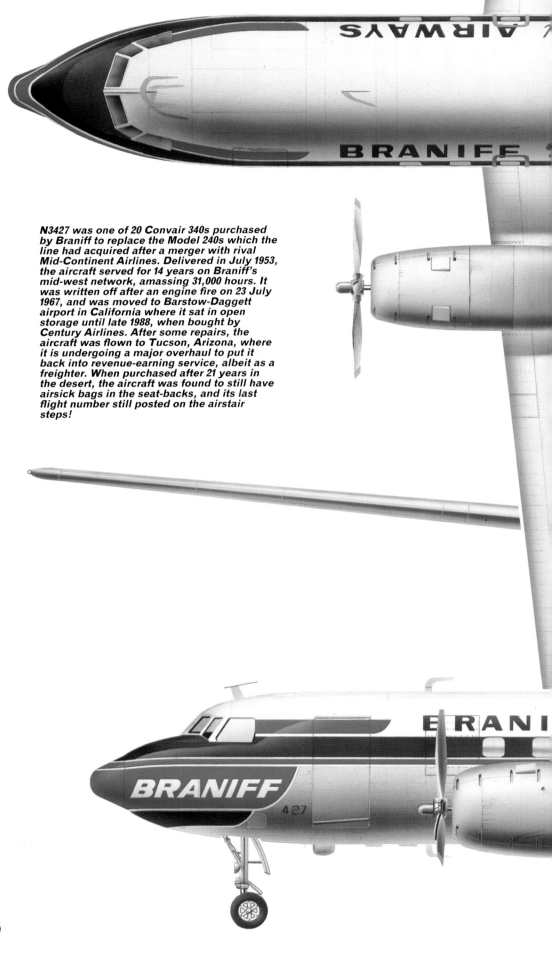

N3427 was one of 20 Convair 340s purchased by Braniff to replace the Model 240s which the line had acquired after a merger with rival Mid-Continent Airlines. Delivered in July 1953, the aircraft served for 14 years on Braniff's mid-west network, amassing 31,000 hours. It was written off after an engine fire on 23 July 1967, and was moved to Barstow-Daggett airport in California where it sat in open storage until late 1988, when bought by Century Airlines. After some repairs, the aircraft was flown to Tucson, Arizona, where it is undergoing a major overhaul to put it back into revenue-earning service, albeit as a freighter. When purchased after 21 years in the desert, the aircraft was found to still have airsick bags in the seat-backs, and its last flight number still posted on the airstair steps!

Specification
Convair 440
Wingspan: 32.1 m (105 ft 4 in)
Length: 24.8 m (81 ft 6 in)
Height: 8.6 m (28 ft 2 in)
Wing area: 85 m² (920 sq ft)
Passenger capacity: 44-52
Empty weight: 15110 kg (33,314 lb)
Payload: 5820 kg (12,836 lb)
Max take-off weight: 22500 kg (49,700 lb)
Cruising speed: 480 km/h (299 mph)
Maximum speed: 540 km/h (337 mph)
Service ceiling: 7590 m (24,900 ft)
Maximum range: 2100 km (1,300 miles)

Specification
Convair 580
Wingspan: 32.1 m (105 ft 4 in)
Length: 24.8 m (81 ft 6 in)
Height: 8.6 m (28 ft 2 in)
Wing area: 85 m² (920 sq ft)
Passenger capacity: 44-56
Max take-off weight: 26400 kg (58,156 lb)
Cruising speed: 560 km/h (352 mph)
Maximum speed: 580 km/h (360 mph)
Maximum range: 4610 km (2,866 miles)

Specification
Convair 640
Wingspan: 32.1 m (105 ft 4 in)
Length: 24.8 m (81 ft 6 in)
Height: 8.6 m (28 ft 2 in)
Wing area: 85 m² (920 sq ft)
Passenger capacity: 44-52
Empty weight: 13730 kg (30,275 lb)
Payload: 7160 kg (15,800 lb)
Max take-off weight: 25000 kg (55,000 lb)
Cruising speed: 480 km/h (300 mph)
Service ceiling: 7600 m (24,900 ft)
Maximum range: 3140 km (1,950 miles)

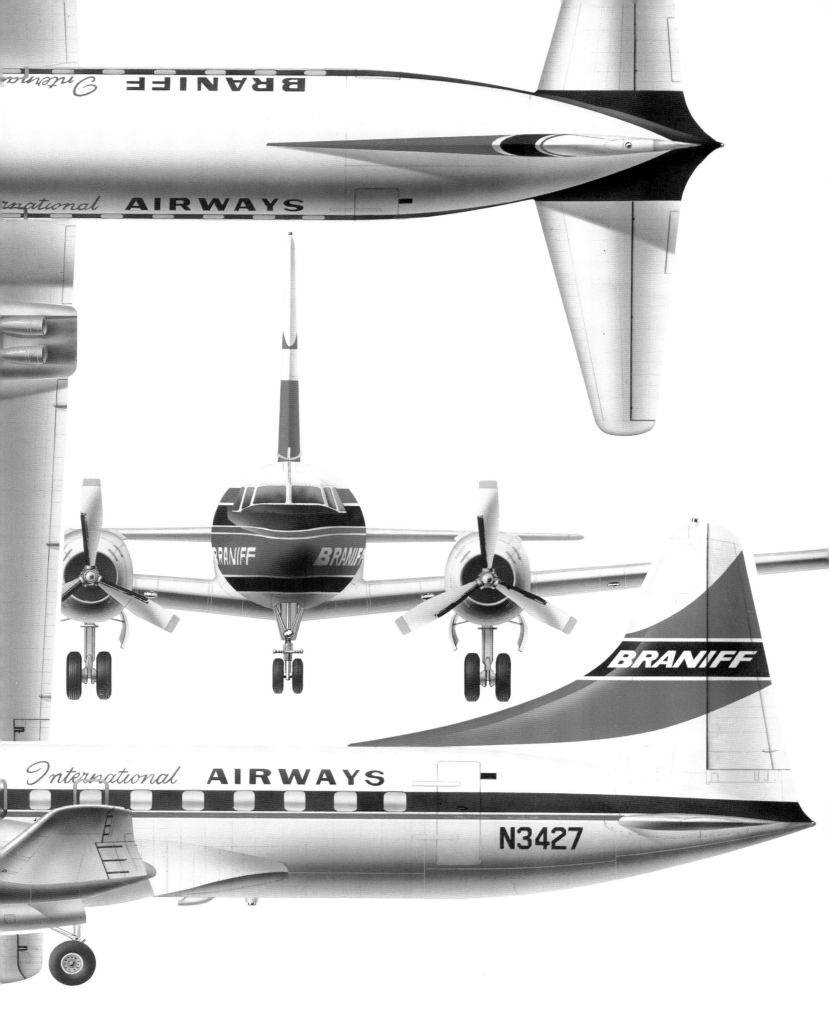

BRANIFF *International* AIRWAYS

International AIRWAYS

BRANIFF

N3427

D.H.106 Comet 4B

One of the best-looking Comet variants, the short-span 4B was derived for British European Airways from the stillborn 4A for the US operator Capital Airlines. Longer than all other versions, it was planned for short-haul European operations, but natural growth in certificated weight endowed it with such range that BEA Airtours and the final operator of the type, Dan-Air, found it an excellent vehicle for long charters and inclusive-tour flights. The aircraft shown was the fifth of BEA's initial batch of six, to which eight more were later added, the only other initial customer being Olympic with four. Interesting features include the bogie main gears with dimpled tyres retracting into bays bulged on the underside, the fatigue-resistant windows and ADF aerials (two black ovals above the forward fuselage), outward-swept jetpipes with Greatrex-type noise-reducing nozzles, and reversers on the outer engines only.

Specification
D.H.106 Comet 4B
Type: medium-range passenger transport
Powerplant: four Rolls-Royce Avon turbojets, originally 4763-kg (10,500-lb) Mk 542; later Mk 525B
Performance: maximum cruising speed 856 km/h (532 mph); typical field length 2134 m (7,000 ft); range with maximum payload (initial weight) 3701 km (2,300 miles), (final weight) 5391 km (3,350 miles)
Weights: empty 33483 kg (73,816 lb); maximum (initial) 69174 kg (152,500 lb) subsequently 70762 kg (156,000 lb) and finally 73483 kg (162,000 lb)
Dimensions: span 32.87 m (107 ft 10 in); length 35.97 m (118 ft 0 in); height 8.69 m (28 ft 6 in); wing area 191.28 m^2 (2,059 sq ft)
Accommodation: flight crew of three or four and normal seating for (initially) 101 passengers, (Dan-Air) 119 passengers

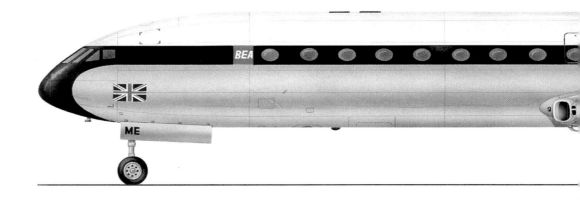

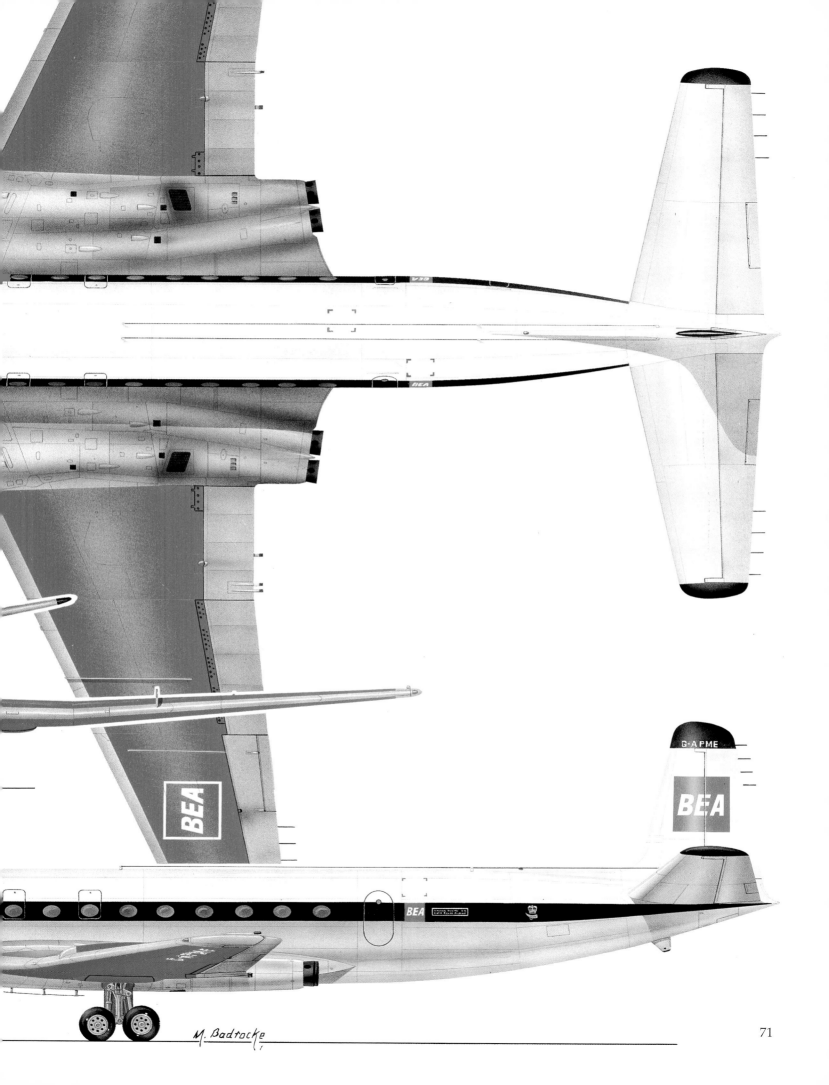

M. Badrocke

NAMC YS-11

One of the many designs tailored to replace the Douglas DC-3 on the networks of domestic airlines, the YS-11 emerged as very similar in configuration to the Avro 748, but with 60 seats was considerably larger. The type sold well in the home market, where Toa, JDA (illustrated) and All Nippon were the main customers, and it continues in service to this day with Japan Air System, the new name for Toa Domestic Airlines, itself a merger between Toa and JDA. JA8648 was the 14th YS-11 built, and the third for JDA. It is not in service today, although the Japan Air Service fleet does include seven YS-11-100s from the original Toa/JDA batches.

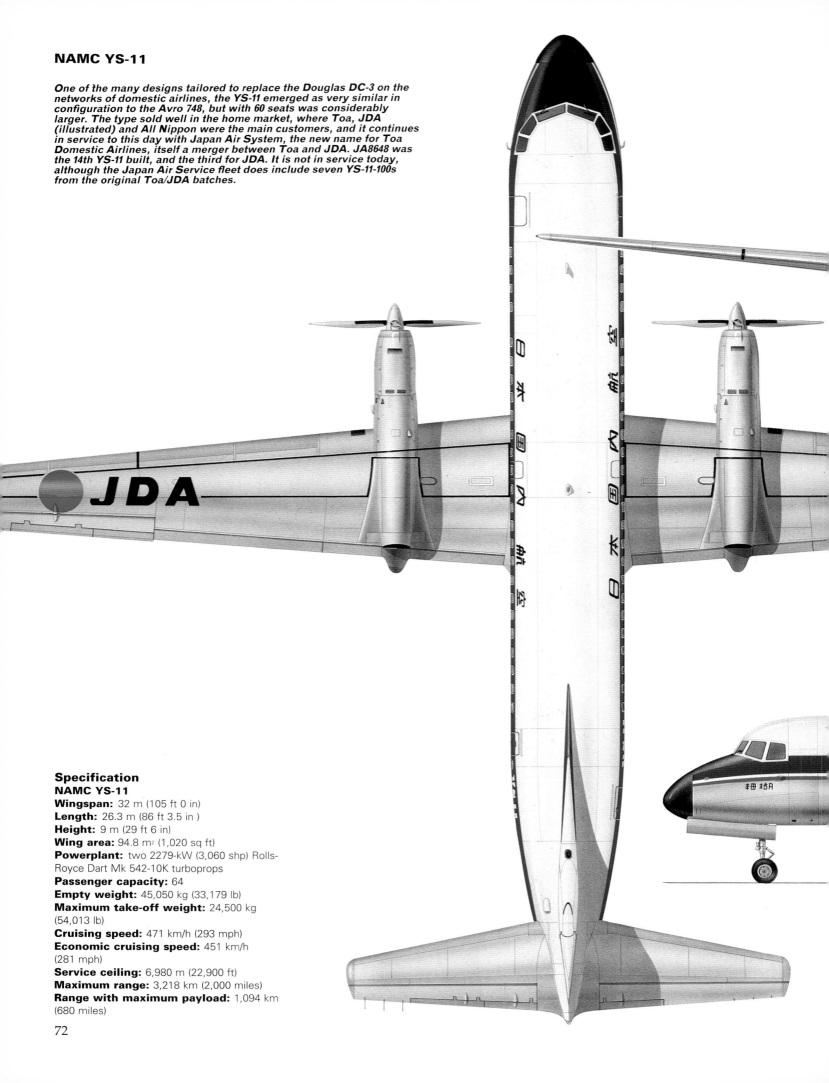

Specification
NAMC YS-11
Wingspan: 32 m (105 ft 0 in)
Length: 26.3 m (86 ft 3.5 in)
Height: 9 m (29 ft 6 in)
Wing area: 94.8 m² (1,020 sq ft)
Powerplant: two 2279-kW (3,060 shp) Rolls-Royce Dart Mk 542-10K turboprops
Passenger capacity: 64
Empty weight: 45,050 kg (33,179 lb)
Maximum take-off weight: 24,500 kg (54,013 lb)
Cruising speed: 471 km/h (293 mph)
Economic cruising speed: 451 km/h (281 mph)
Service ceiling: 6,980 m (22,900 ft)
Maximum range: 3,218 km (2,000 miles)
Range with maximum payload: 1,094 km (680 miles)

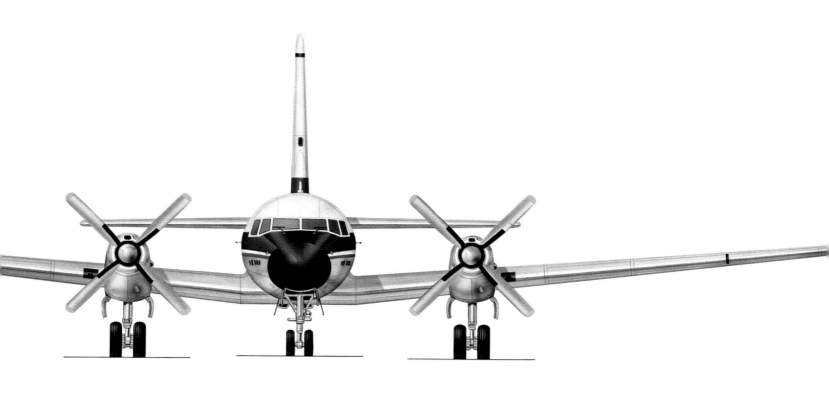

JA8648

Mike Badrocke

Vickers Vanguard Type 952

G-APEE 'Euryalus' was the penultimate Vanguard 951 built for British European Airways. Vickers introduced the V.953 from the seventh production aircraft, certifying it for operations at a higher gross weight over a slightly shorter range than the V.951. When BEA learned of these plans it changed its order to six V.951s and 14 V.953s, production being too far advanced to revise the initial half dozen. Vanguards entered service on route-proving trials in February 1960, but in the final week of trials service entry was formally delayed by a hitch with the power supply unit. BEA had planned a summer service with the Vanguard and was extremely unhappy with the delay. Problems were resolved by December, however, and G-APEE was used extensively for crew-training at Stansted from the second of the month onwards. Sadly Euryalus was to have a short career with BEA. Delivered in early December 1960, 'Euryalus' was lost when it overshot the runway and crashed, in fog, at Heathrow on 27 October 1965.

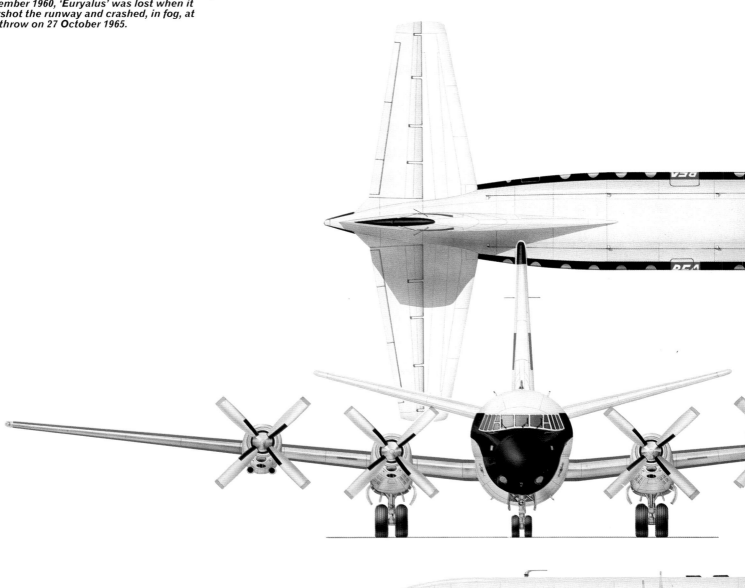

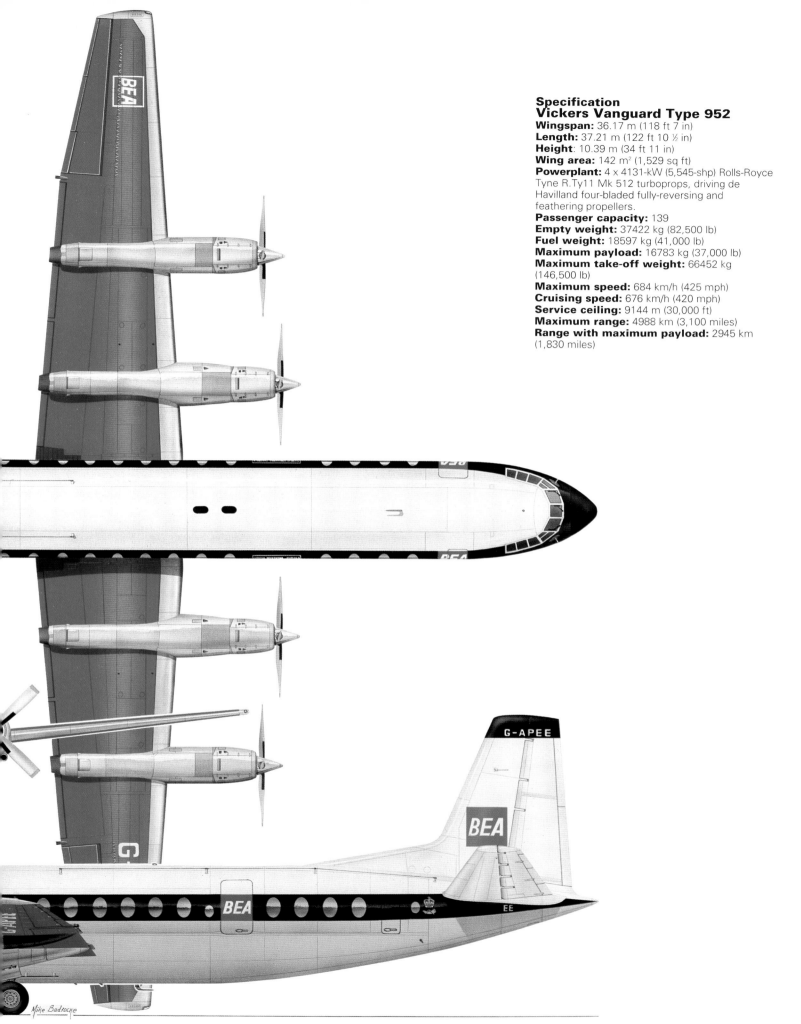

Specification
Vickers Vanguard Type 952
Wingspan: 36.17 m (118 ft 7 in)
Length: 37.21 m (122 ft 10 ½ in)
Height: 10.39 m (34 ft 11 in)
Wing area: 142 m² (1,529 sq ft)
Powerplant: 4 x 4131-kW (5,545-shp) Rolls-Royce Tyne R.Ty11 Mk 512 turboprops, driving de Havilland four-bladed fully-reversing and feathering propellers.
Passenger capacity: 139
Empty weight: 37422 kg (82,500 lb)
Fuel weight: 18597 kg (41,000 lb)
Maximum payload: 16783 kg (37,000 lb)
Maximum take-off weight: 66452 kg (146,500 lb)
Maximum speed: 684 km/h (425 mph)
Cruising speed: 676 km/h (420 mph)
Service ceiling: 9144 m (30,000 ft)
Maximum range: 4988 km (3,100 miles)
Range with maximum payload: 2945 km (1,830 miles)

Mike Badrocke

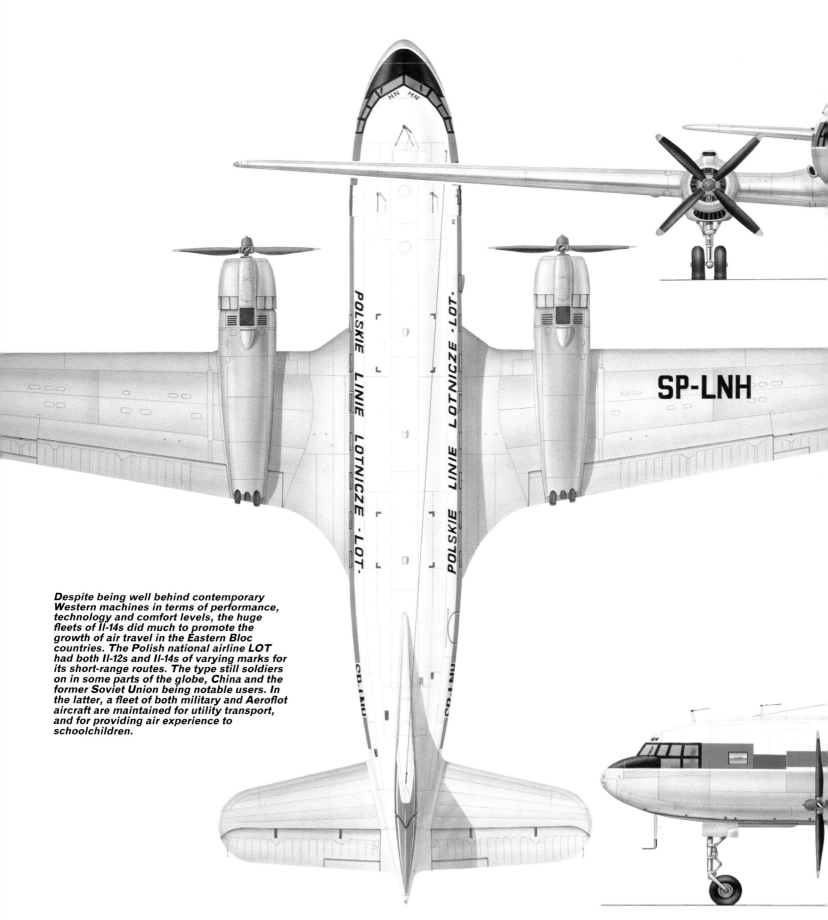

Despite being well behind contemporary Western machines in terms of performance, technology and comfort levels, the huge fleets of Il-14s did much to promote the growth of air travel in the Eastern Bloc countries. The Polish national airline *LOT* had both Il-12s and Il-14s of varying marks for its short-range routes. The type still soldiers on in some parts of the globe, China and the former Soviet Union being notable users. In the latter, a fleet of both military and Aeroflot aircraft are maintained for utility transport, and for providing air experience to schoolchildren.

POLSKIE LINIE LOTNICZE ·LOT·

SP-LNH

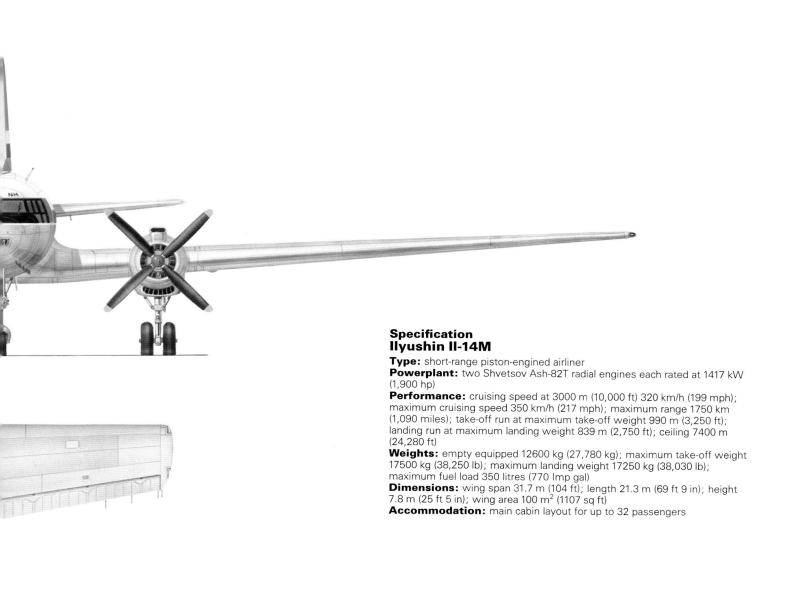

Specification
Ilyushin Il-14M

Type: short-range piston-engined airliner
Powerplant: two Shvetsov Ash-82T radial engines each rated at 1417 kW (1,900 hp)
Performance: cruising speed at 3000 m (10,000 ft) 320 km/h (199 mph); maximum cruising speed 350 km/h (217 mph); maximum range 1750 km (1,090 miles); take-off run at maximum take-off weight 990 m (3,250 ft); landing run at maximum landing weight 839 m (2,750 ft); ceiling 7400 m (24,280 ft)
Weights: empty equipped 12600 kg (27,780 kg); maximum take-off weight 17500 kg (38,250 lb); maximum landing weight 17250 kg (38,030 lb); maximum fuel load 350 litres (770 Imp gal)
Dimensions: wing span 31.7 m (104 ft); length 21.3 m (69 ft 9 in); height 7.8 m (25 ft 5 in); wing area 100 m^2 (1107 sq ft)
Accommodation: main cabin layout for up to 32 passengers

POLSKIE LINIE LOTNICZE ·LOT·

SP-LNH

Mike Badrocke

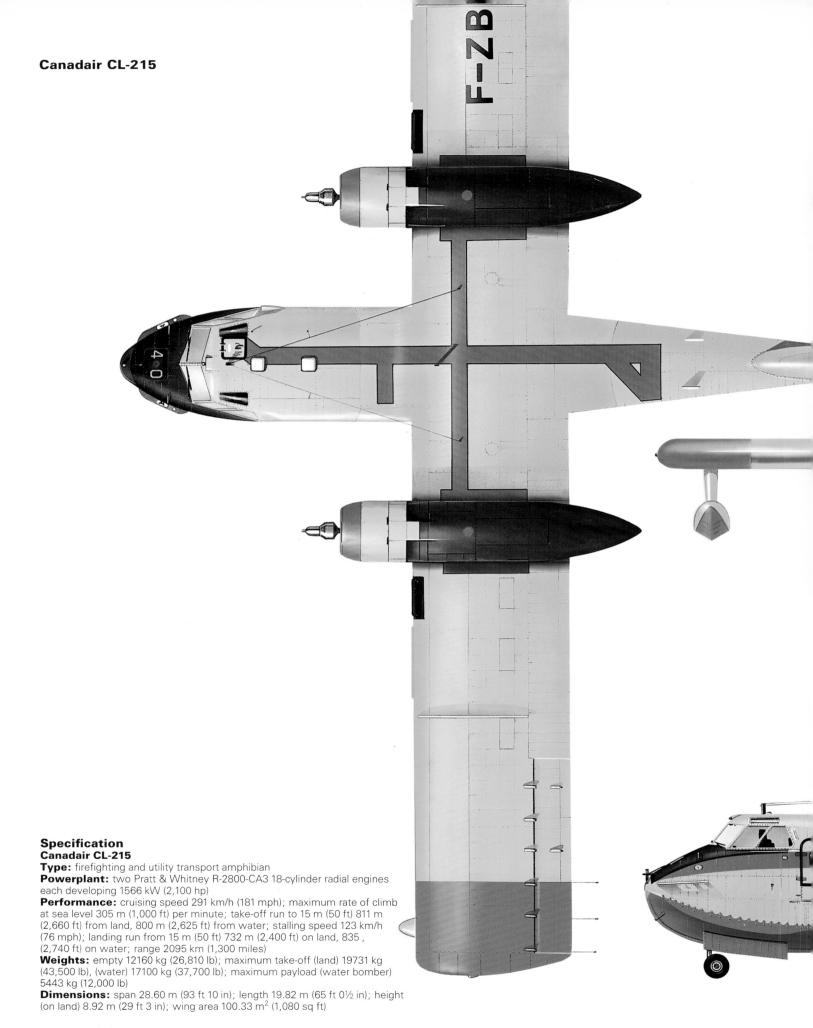

Canadair CL-215

Specification
Canadair CL-215
Type: firefighting and utility transport amphibian
Powerplant: two Pratt & Whitney R-2800-CA3 18-cylinder radial engines each developing 1566 kW (2,100 hp)
Performance: cruising speed 291 km/h (181 mph); maximum rate of climb at sea level 305 m (1,000 ft) per minute; take-off run to 15 m (50 ft) 811 m (2,660 ft) from land, 800 m (2,625 ft) from water; stalling speed 123 km/h (76 mph); landing run from 15 m (50 ft) 732 m (2,400 ft) on land, 835 , (2,740 ft) on water; range 2095 km (1,300 miles)
Weights: empty 12160 kg (26,810 lb); maximum take-off (land) 19731 kg (43,500 lb), (water) 17100 kg (37,700 lb); maximum payload (water bomber) 5443 kg (12,000 lb)
Dimensions: span 28.60 m (93 ft 10 in); length 19.82 m (65 ft 0½ in); height (on land) 8.92 m (29 ft 3 in); wing area 100.33 m² (1,080 sq ft)

The *Canadair CL-215* is designed around the swift extinguishing of forest fires at a practical cost. At the heart of the machine are the water tanks, which can accommodate 5346 litres of water. These are filled as the aircraft skims across a lake or river, two scoops projecting into the water from the hull and using ram pressure to fill the tanks in about 10 seconds. Once the filling is complete, the scoops are retracted and the aircraft climbs away. Over the drop site, large doors are opened to dump the full load in a second. The new turboprop-powered *CL-215T* features two sets of doors to allow the water to be dumped in salvo (all at one time) or in train (one set preceding the other), this giving a variable spread pattern.

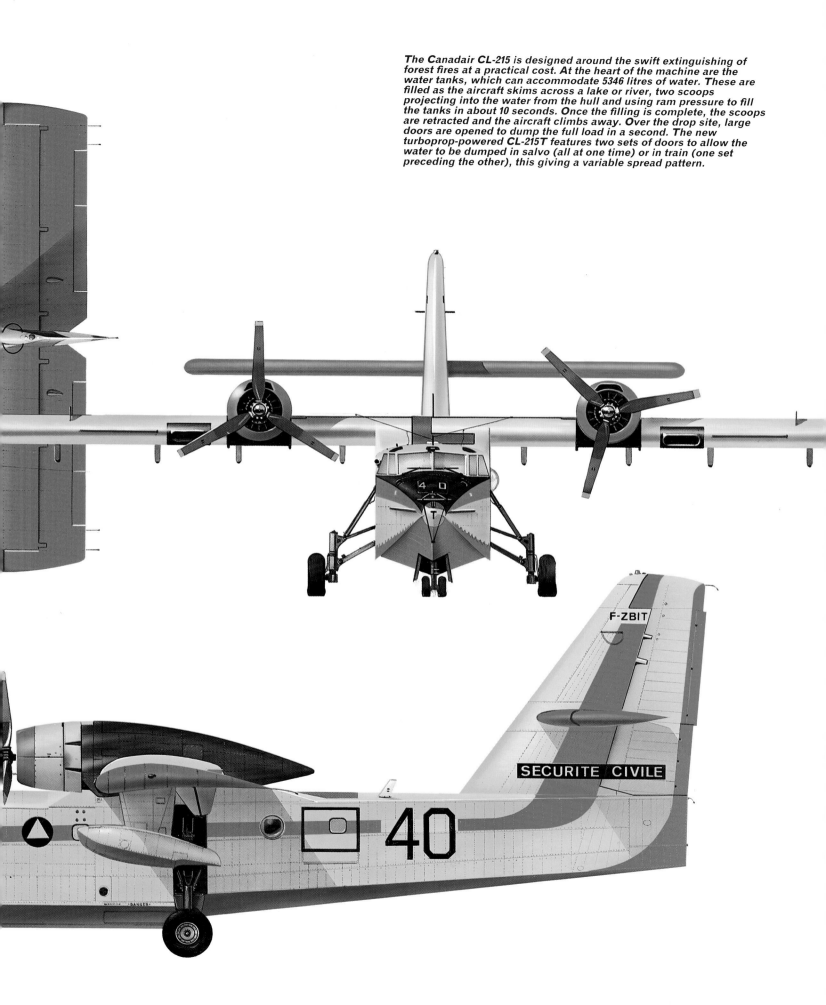

F-ZBIT

SECURITE CIVILE

40

BAC (Vickers) Type 1151 Super VC10

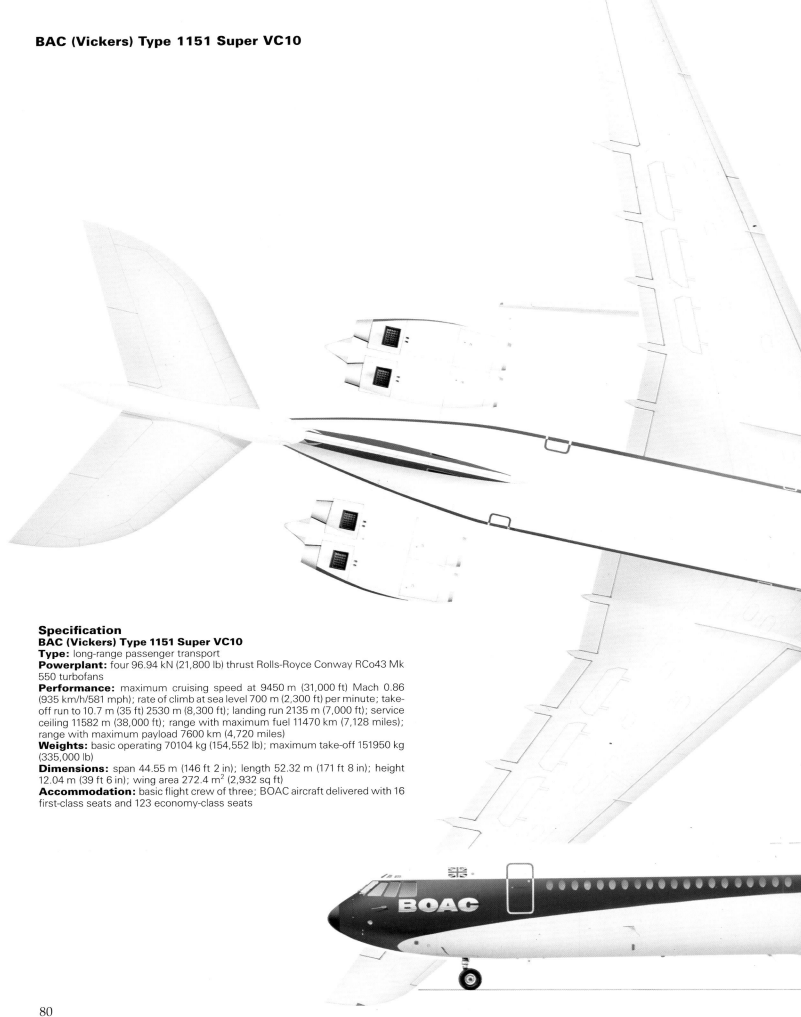

Specification
BAC (Vickers) Type 1151 Super VC10
Type: long-range passenger transport

Powerplant: four 96.94 kN (21,800 lb) thrust Rolls-Royce Conway RCo43 Mk 550 turbofans

Performance: maximum cruising speed at 9450 m (31,000 ft) Mach 0.86 (935 km/h/581 mph); rate of climb at sea level 700 m (2,300 ft) per minute; take-off run to 10.7 m (35 ft) 2530 m (8,300 ft); landing run 2135 m (7,000 ft); service ceiling 11582 m (38,000 ft); range with maximum fuel 11470 km (7,128 miles); range with maximum payload 7600 km (4,720 miles)

Weights: basic operating 70104 kg (154,552 lb); maximum take-off 151950 kg (335,000 lb)

Dimensions: span 44.55 m (146 ft 2 in); length 52.32 m (171 ft 8 in); height 12.04 m (39 ft 6 in); wing area 272.4 m^2 (2,932 sq ft)

Accommodation: basic flight crew of three; BOAC aircraft delivered with 16 first-class seats and 123 economy-class seats

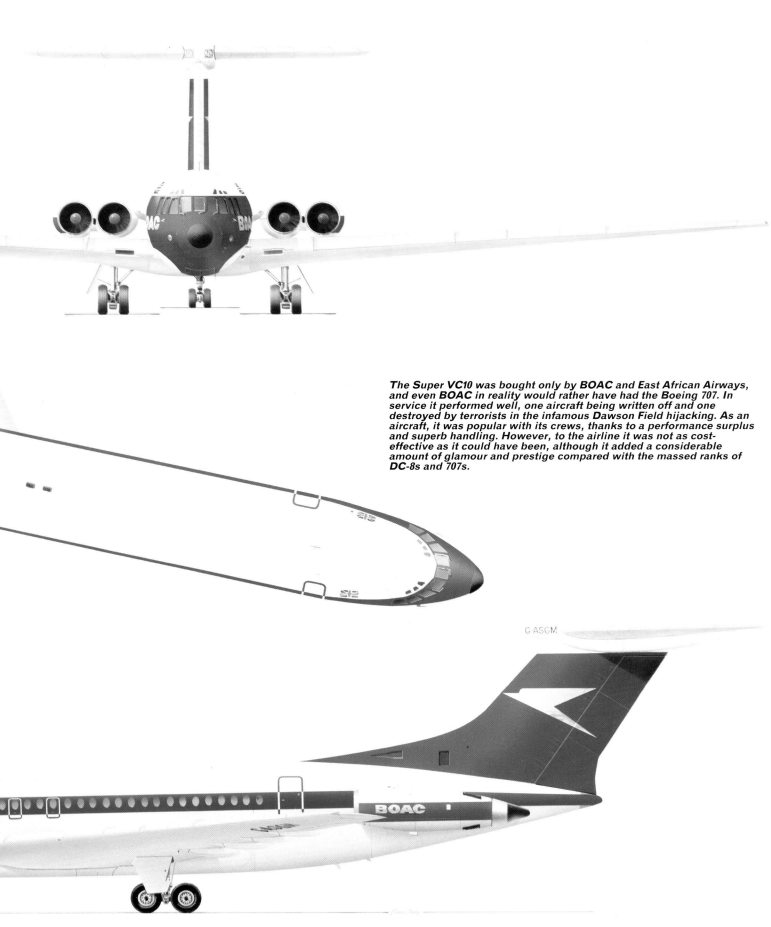

The Super VC10 was bought only by **BOAC** and East African Airways, and even **BOAC** in reality would rather have had the Boeing 707. In service it performed well, one aircraft being written off and one destroyed by terrorists in the infamous Dawson Field hijacking. As an aircraft, it was popular with its crews, thanks to a performance surplus and superb handling. However, to the airline it was not as cost-effective as it could have been, although it added a considerable amount of glamour and prestige compared with the massed ranks of **DC**-8s and 707s.

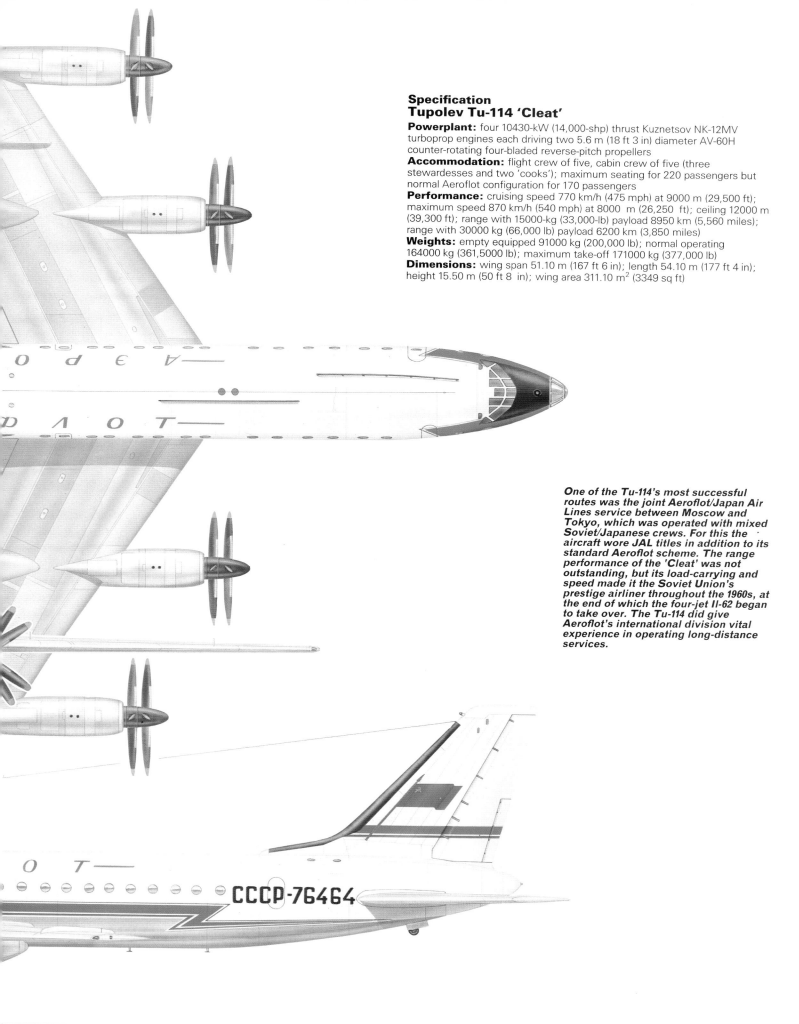

Specification
Tupolev Tu-114 'Cleat'

Powerplant: four 10430-kW (14,000-shp) thrust Kuznetsov NK-12MV turboprop engines each driving two 5.6 m (18 ft 3 in) diameter AV-60H counter-rotating four-bladed reverse-pitch propellers

Accommodation: flight crew of five, cabin crew of five (three stewardesses and two 'cooks'); maximum seating for 220 passengers but normal Aeroflot configuration for 170 passengers

Performance: cruising speed 770 km/h (475 mph) at 9000 m (29,500 ft); maximum speed 870 km/h (540 mph) at 8000 m (26,250 ft); ceiling 12000 m (39,300 ft); range with 15000-kg (33,000-lb) payload 8950 km (5,560 miles); range with 30000 kg (66,000 lb) payload 6200 km (3,850 miles)

Weights: empty equipped 91000 kg (200,000 lb); normal operating 164000 kg (361,5000 lb); maximum take-off 171000 kg (377,000 lb)

Dimensions: wing span 51.10 m (167 ft 6 in); length 54.10 m (177 ft 4 in); height 15.50 m (50 ft 8 in); wing area 311.10 m² (3349 sq ft)

One of the Tu-114's most successful routes was the joint Aeroflot/Japan Air Lines service between Moscow and Tokyo, which was operated with mixed Soviet/Japanese crews. For this the aircraft wore JAL titles in addition to its standard Aeroflot scheme. The range performance of the 'Cleat' was not outstanding, but its load-carrying and speed made it the Soviet Union's prestige airliner throughout the 1960s, at the end of which the four-jet Il-62 began to take over. The Tu-114 did give Aeroflot's international division vital experience in operating long-distance services.

CCCP-76464

LET L-410UVP-E Turbolet

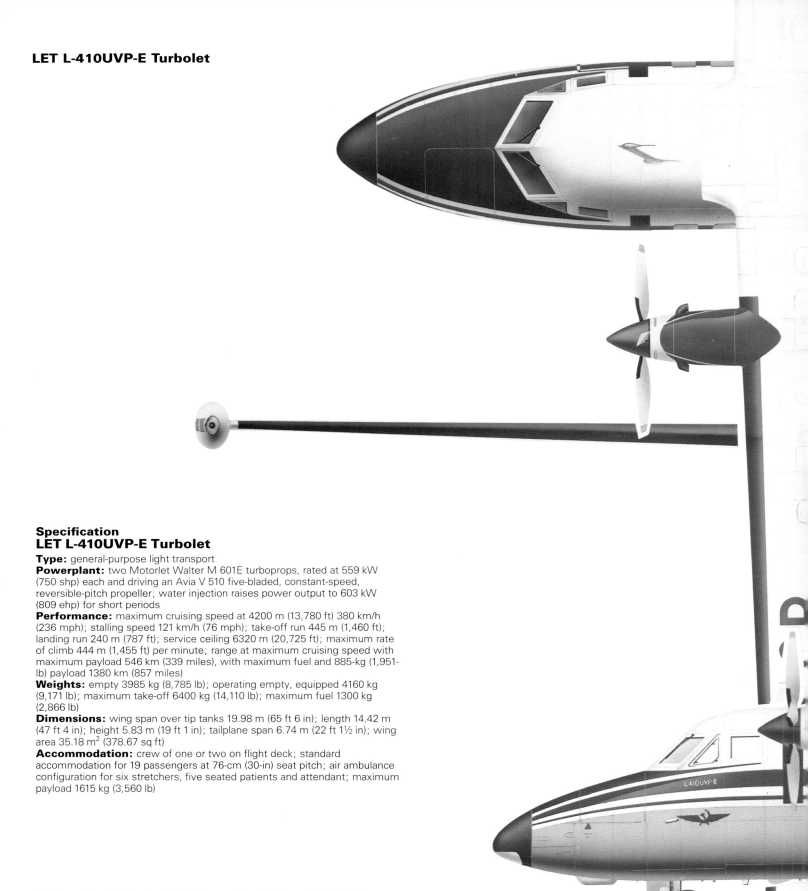

Specification
LET L-410UVP-E Turbolet

Type: general-purpose light transport

Powerplant: two Motorlet Walter M 601E turboprops, rated at 559 kW (750 shp) each and driving an Avia V 510 five-bladed, constant-speed, reversible-pitch propeller; water injection raises power output to 603 kW (809 ehp) for short periods

Performance: maximum cruising speed at 4200 m (13,780 ft) 380 km/h (236 mph); stalling speed 121 km/h (76 mph); take-off run 445 m (1,460 ft); landing run 240 m (787 ft); service ceiling 6320 m (20,725 ft); maximum rate of climb 444 m (1,455 ft) per minute; range at maximum cruising speed with maximum payload 546 km (339 miles), with maximum fuel and 885-kg (1,951-lb) payload 1380 km (857 miles)

Weights: empty 3985 kg (8,785 lb); operating empty, equipped 4160 kg (9,171 lb); maximum take-off 6400 kg (14,110 lb); maximum fuel 1300 kg (2,866 lb)

Dimensions: wing span over tip tanks 19.98 m (65 ft 6 in); length 14.42 m (47 ft 4 in); height 5.83 m (19 ft 1 in); tailplane span 6.74 m (22 ft 1½ in); wing area 35.18 m^2 (378.67 sq ft)

Accommodation: crew of one or two on flight deck; standard accommodation for 19 passengers at 76-cm (30-in) seat pitch; air ambulance configuration for six stretchers, five seated patients and attendant; maximum payload 1615 kg (3,560 lb)

Distinguished by its five-bladed propeller, this is an L-410UVP-E, wearing the colours of Aeroflot. The Czech type serves alongside the Soviet-designed but Polish-built Antonov An-28 on regional routes within the former Soviet Union. Internal rearrangements mean the UVP-E can carry 19 passengers instead of the previous 15, while it can also perform light cargo transport and air ambulance work. Stringent Aeroflot requirements dictate an operational envelope embracing a temperature range of −50C to +50C.

СССР-67551

CCCP-67551

CCCP-67551

ЭРОФЛОТ

Canadair CL-44D4

The CL-44D4-2s delivered to the Flying Tiger Line in 1961/62 were supplied without cabin windows, being tailored to the carrier's extensive cargo network from the outset. The Britannia lineage is obvious, but the CL-44 was considerably more powerful and capable. The swing tail allowed bulky cargo to be loaded swiftly, although the aircraft retained their standard forward fuselage side cargo doors. This particular machine was delivered on 31 May 1961, and was later the sole subject of the CL-44-O conversion, flying again in this configuration on 26 November 1969.

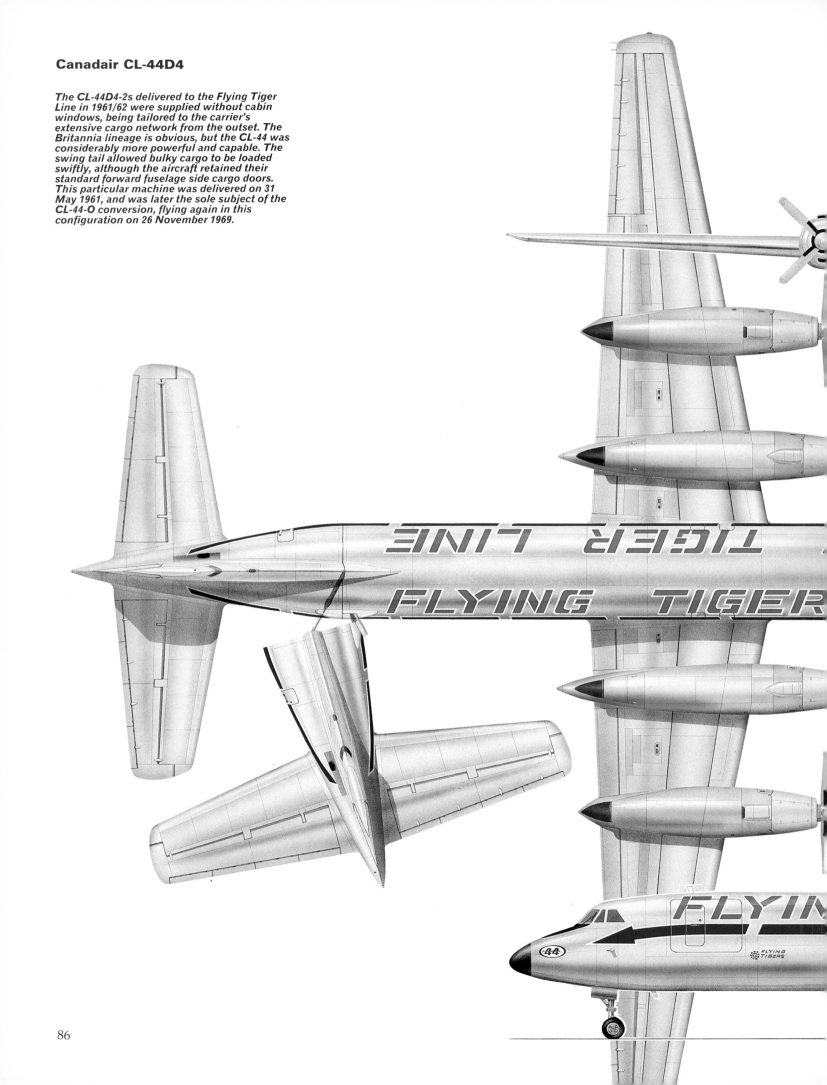

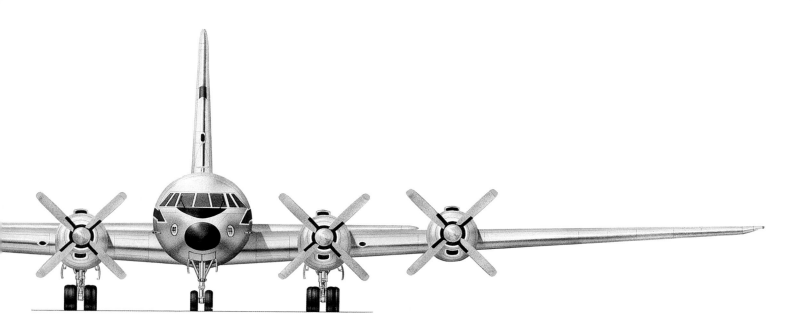

Specification
Canadair CL-44D4

Wingspan: 43.38 m (142 ft 3½ in)
Length: 41.73(136 ft 10¾ in)
Height: 11.76 m (38 ft 7 in)
Wing area: 192.76 m² (2,075 sq ft)
Powerplant: four 4275-kW (5,730-shp) Rolls-Royce Tyne Mk. 515/10 turboprops
Empty weight: 40349 kg (88,952 lb)
Maximum take-off weight: 95256 kg (210,000 lb)
Passenger capacity: 178
Maximum speed: 621 km/h (386 mph)
Cruising speed: 464 km/h (288 mph)
Service ceiling: 9144 m(30,000 ft)
Maximum range: 8991 km (5,587 miles)
Range with maximum payload: 5246 km (3,260 miles)

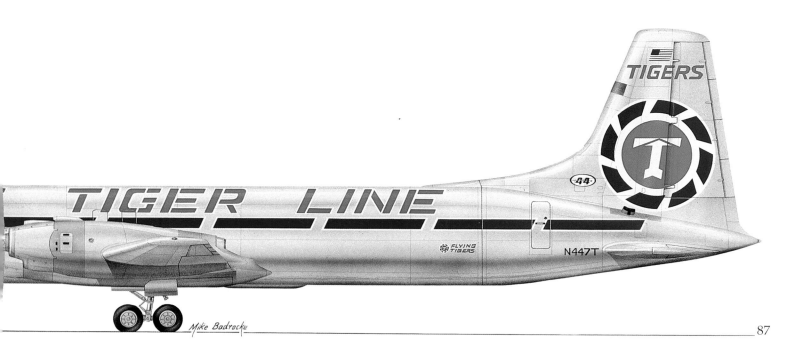

Mike Badrocke

Ilyushin Il-18

One of a crop of four-engined turboprops that included the Britannia, Vanguard and Electra, the Il-18 proved to be the longest-lived. Still in widespread service with operators in less-developed nations, the Il-18 has a typically Soviet reputation for ruggedness and simplicity of operation. China is one of the current operators, including this AI-20M-powered aircraft in its remaining fleet. As the emerging Communist nation undergoes a radical modernisation of its civil aviation fleet, the days of elderly aircraft such as the Il-18 are numbered.

Specification
Ilyushin Il-18
Type: medium-range transport
Powerplant: four Ivchenko AI-20K or AI-20M turboprops, developing 2983 kW (4,000 ehp) and 3169 kW (4,250 ehp) respectively
Performance: maximum cruising speed (Il-18V) 650 km/h (404 mph), (Il-18D/E) 675 km/h (419 mph); operating height 10000 m (32,800 ft); take-off run (Il-180) 1300 m (4,265 ft), (Il-18E) 1100 m (3,610 ft); range with maximum fuel (Il-18D) 6500 km (4,040 miles), (Il-18E) 5200 km (3,230 miles); range with maximum payload (Il-18D) 3700 km (2,300 miles), (Il-18E) 3200 km (1,990 miles)
Weights: empty equipped (Il-18D) 35000 kg (77,160 lb), (Il-18E) 34630 kg (76,350 lb); maximum take-off (Il-18D) 64000 kg (141,100 lb), (Il-18E,V) 61200 kg (134,925 lb)
Dimensions: span 37.40 m (122 ft 8½ in); length 35.90 m (117 ft 9 in); height 10.17 m (33 ft 4 in); wing area 140 m² (1,507 sq ft)

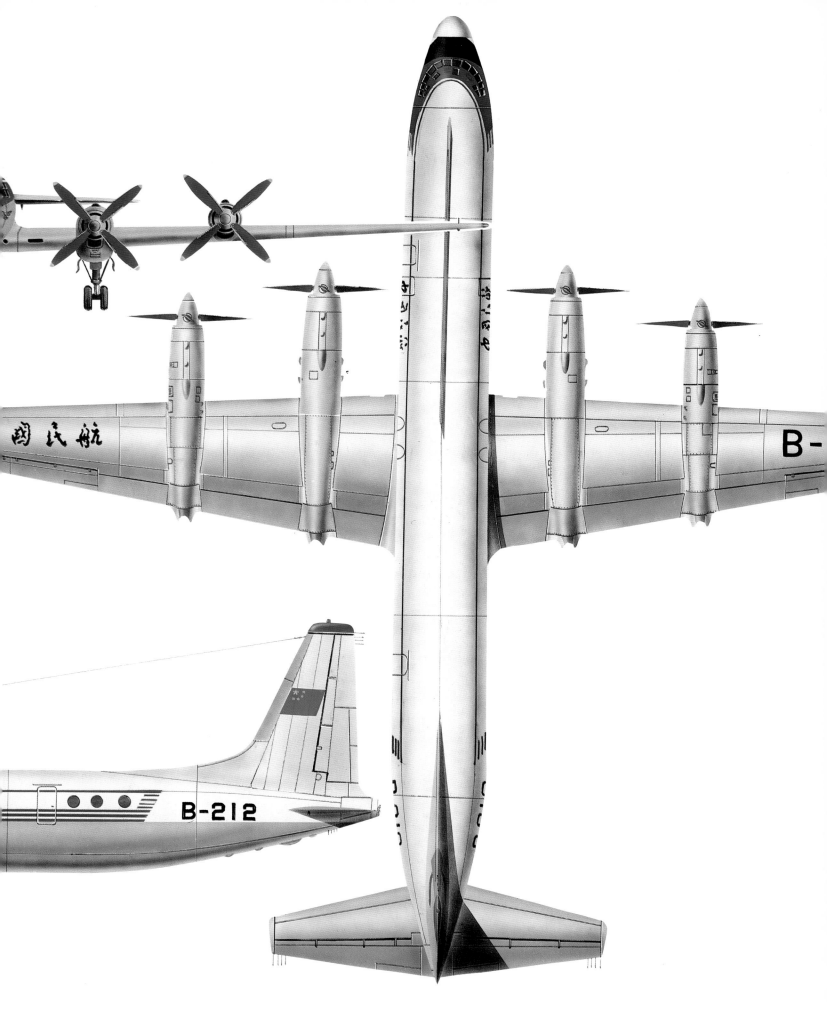

B-212

中國民航

B-

Boeing Model 707-321B

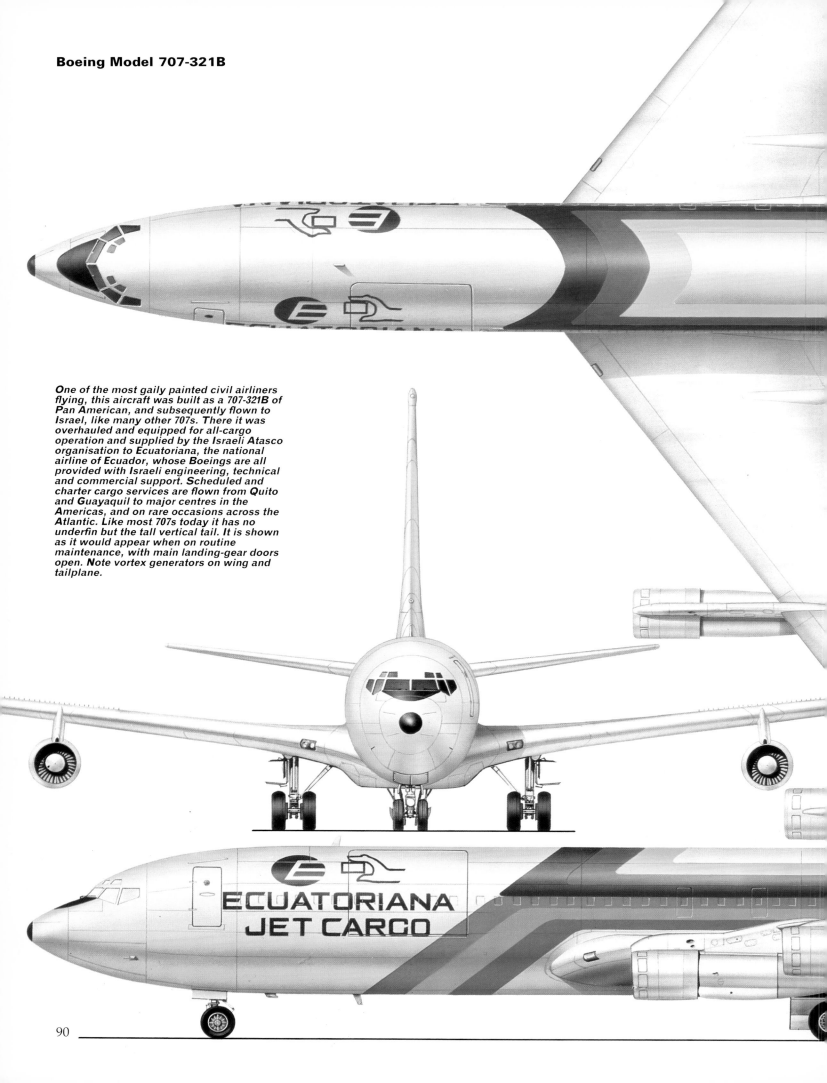

One of the most gaily painted civil airliners flying, this aircraft was built as a 707-321B of Pan American, and subsequently flown to Israel, like many other 707s. There it was overhauled and equipped for all-cargo operation and supplied by the Israeli Atasco organisation to Ecuatoriana, the national airline of Ecuador, whose Boeings are all provided with Israeli engineering, technical and commercial support. Scheduled and charter cargo services are flown from Quito and Guayaquil to major centres in the Americas, and on rare occasions across the Atlantic. Like most 707s today it has no underfin but the tall vertical tail. It is shown as it would appear when on routine maintenance, with main landing-gear doors open. Note vortex generators on wing and tailplane.

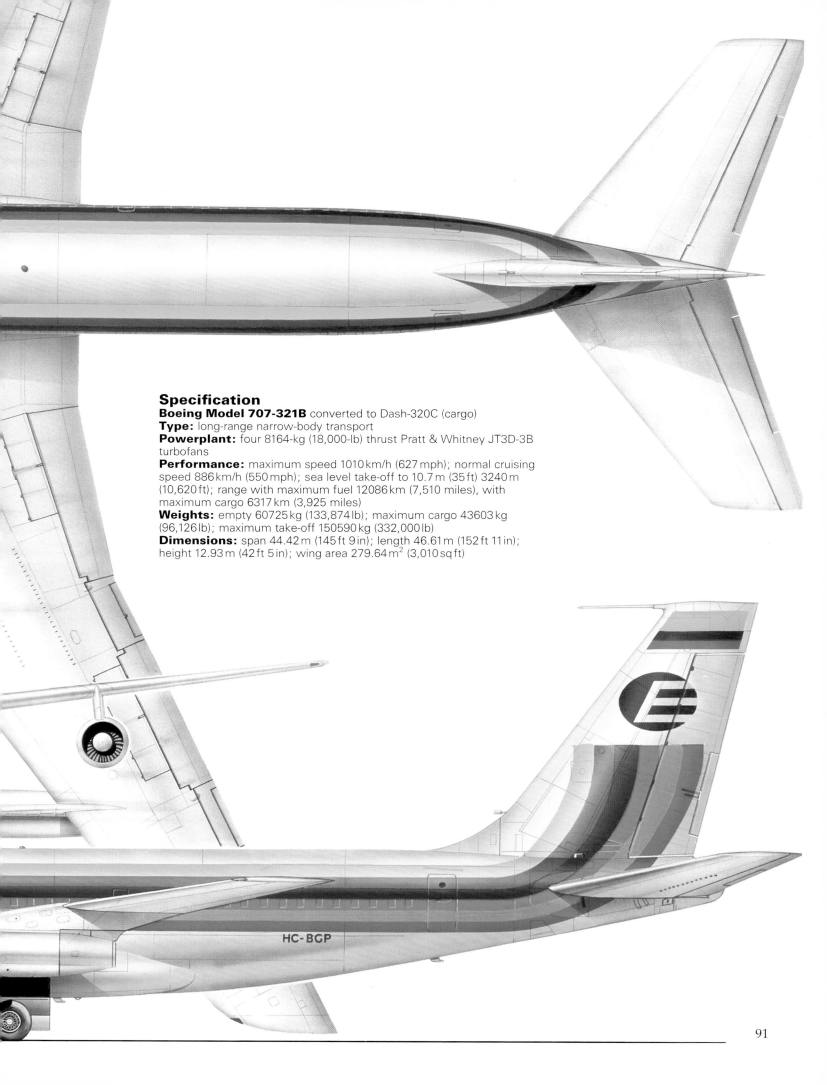

Specification

Boeing Model 707-321B converted to Dash-320C (cargo)

Type: long-range narrow-body transport

Powerplant: four 8164-kg (18,000-lb) thrust Pratt & Whitney JT3D-3B turbofans

Performance: maximum speed 1010 km/h (627 mph); normal cruising speed 886 km/h (550 mph); sea level take-off to 10.7 m (35 ft) 3240 m (10,620 ft); range with maximum fuel 12086 km (7,510 miles), with maximum cargo 6317 km (3,925 miles)

Weights: empty 60725 kg (133,874 lb); maximum cargo 43603 kg (96,126 lb); maximum take-off 150590 kg (332,000 lb)

Dimensions: span 44.42 m (145 ft 9 in); length 46.61 m (152 ft 11 in); height 12.93 m (42 ft 5 in); wing area 279.64 m^2 (3,010 sq ft)

HC-BGP

Rockwell Thrush Commander

Specification
Rockwell Thrush Commander

Type: single-seat agricultural aircraft
Powerplant: one 600-hp Pratt & Whitney R-1340-AN-1 or -S3H1 nine-cylinder radial aircooled piston engine.
Performance: max level speed 225 km/h (140 mph); cruising speed 177 km/h (110 mph); stalling speed, flaps up normal weight 89 km/h (55 mph)
Dimensions: wing span 13.54 m (44 ft 5 in); length overall 8.95 m (29 ft 4½ in); height 2.79 m (9 ft 2 in)
Weights: empty, equipped 1791 kg (3,950 lb); maximum take-off weight 3130 kg (6,900 lb)

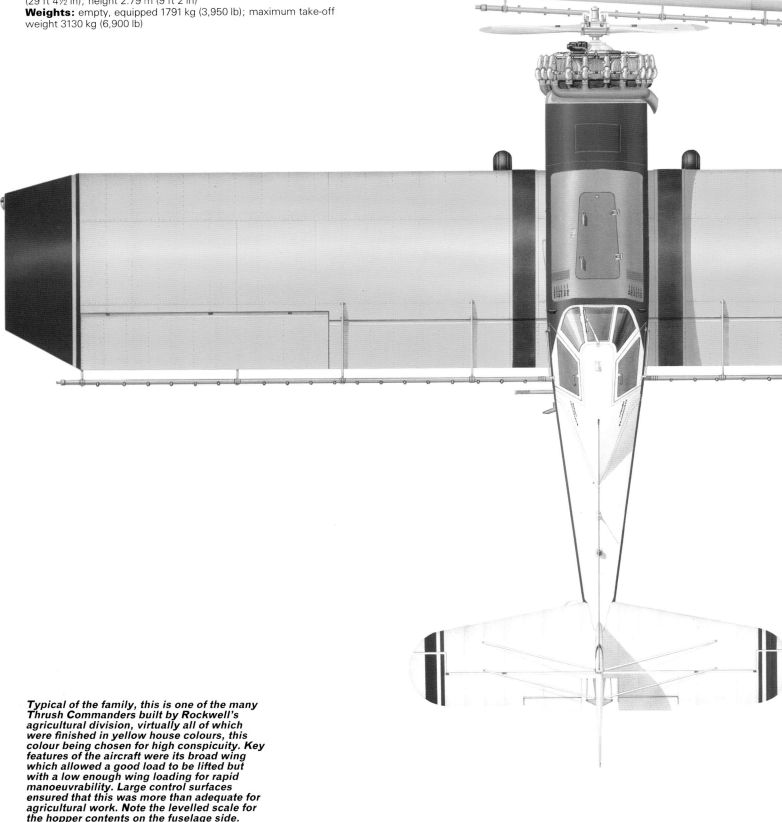

Typical of the family, this is one of the many Thrush Commanders built by Rockwell's agricultural division, virtually all of which were finished in yellow house colours, this colour being chosen for high conspicuity. Key features of the aircraft were its broad wing which allowed a good load to be lifted but with a low enough wing loading for rapid manoeuvrability. Large control surfaces ensured that this was more than adequate for agricultural work. Note the levelled scale for the hopper contents on the fuselage side.

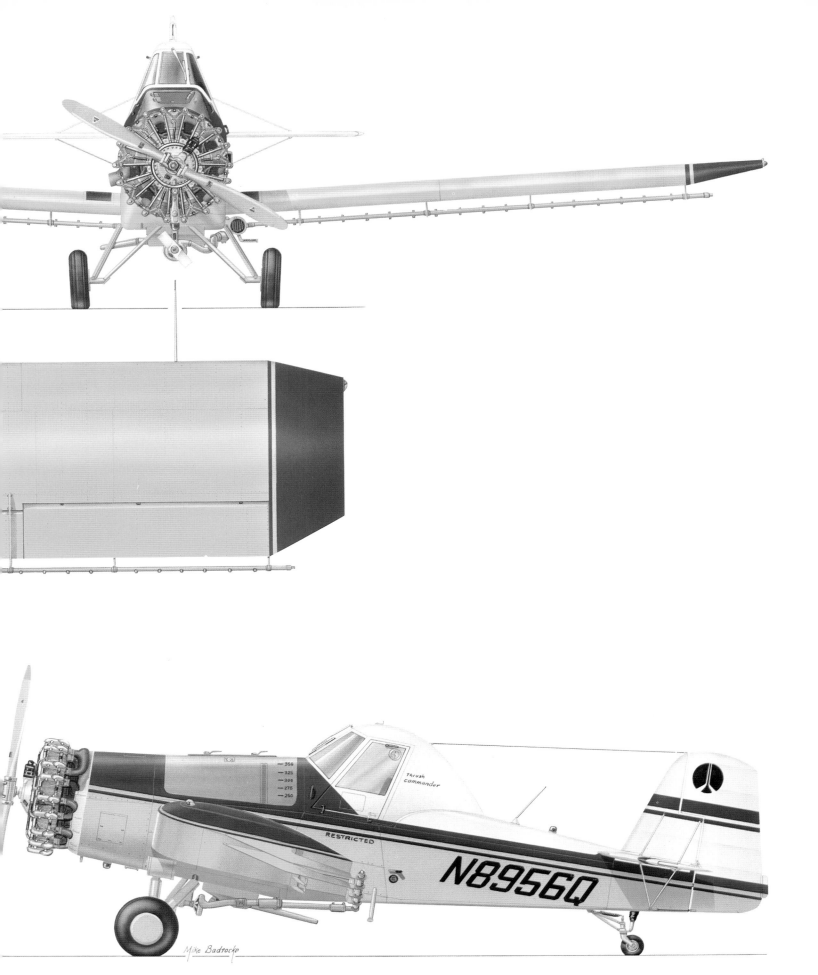

Mike Badtocke

Thrush
Commander

RESTRICTED

N8956Q

Martin 2-0-2/4-0-4

Specification
Martin 2-0-2
Wing span: 28.4 m (93 ft 3 in)
Length: 21.7 m (71 ft 4 in)
Height: 8.6 m (28 ft 5 in)
Wing area: 80.2 m^2 (864 sq ft)
Passenger capacity: 32-40
Empty weight: 11379 kg (25,086 lb)
Payload: 6719 kg (14,814 lb)
Maximum take-off weight: 18098 kg (39,900 lb)
Cruising speed: 445 km/h (277 mph)
Maximum speed: 492 km/h (306 mph)
Service ceiling: 6888 m (22,600 ft)
Maximum range: 2510 km (1,560 miles)

Specification
Martin 4-0-4
Wing span: 28.4 m (93 ft 3 in)
Length: 22.7 m (74 ft 7 in)
Height: 8.6 m (28 ft 5 in)
Wing area: 80.2 m^2 (864 sq ft)
Passenger capacity: 40
Empty weight: 13211 kg (29,126 lb)
Maximum take-off weight: 20366 kg (44,900 lb)
Cruising speed: 450.7 km/h (280 mph)
Maximum speed: 502.4 km/h (312 mph)
Service ceiling: 8839 m (29,000 ft)
Range with maximum payload: 1488 km (925 miles)
Maximum range: 4185 km (2,600 miles)

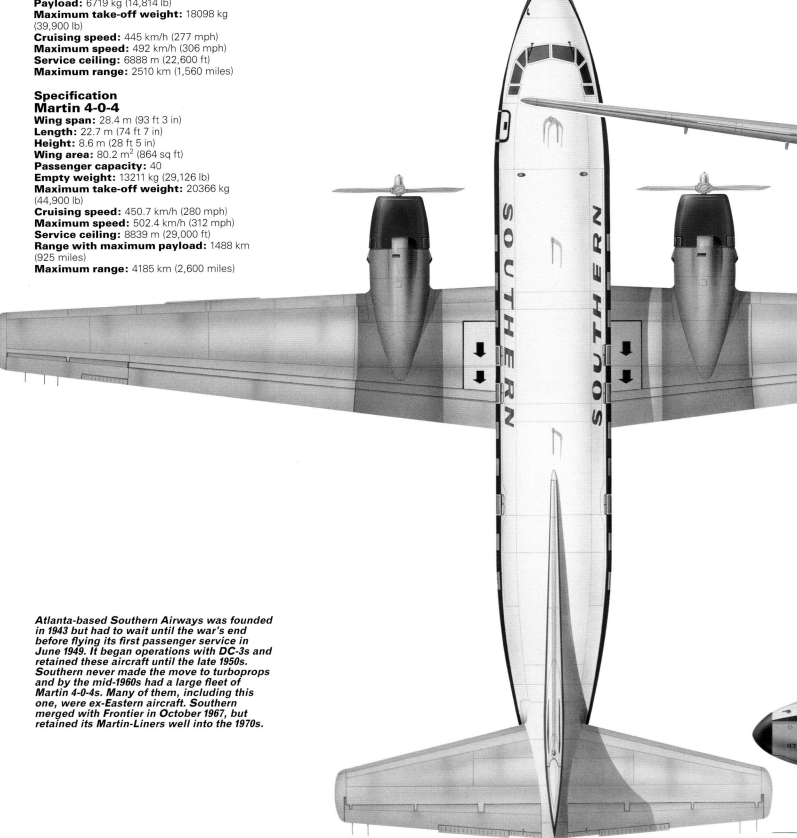

Atlanta-based Southern Airways was founded in 1943 but had to wait until the war's end before flying its first passenger service in June 1949. It began operations with DC-3s and retained these aircraft until the late 1950s. Southern never made the move to turboprops and by the mid-1960s had a large fleet of Martin 4-0-4s. Many of them, including this one, were ex-Eastern aircraft. Southern merged with Frontier in October 1967, but retained its Martin-Liners well into the 1970s.

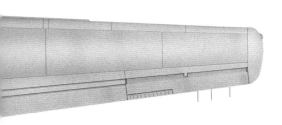

Mike Badtocke

Bristol Type 175 Britannia Series 310

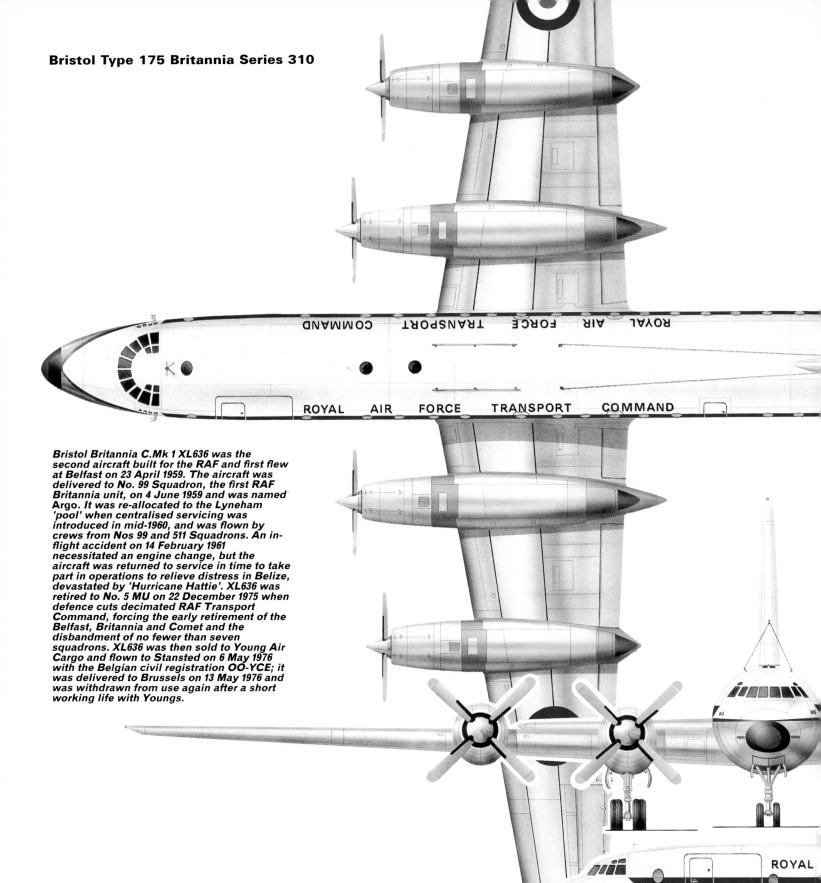

Bristol Britannia C.Mk 1 XL636 was the second aircraft built for the RAF and first flew at Belfast on 23 April 1959. The aircraft was delivered to No. 99 Squadron, the first RAF Britannia unit, on 4 June 1959 and was named Argo. It was re-allocated to the Lyneham 'pool' when centralised servicing was introduced in mid-1960, and was flown by crews from Nos 99 and 511 Squadrons. An in-flight accident on 14 February 1961 necessitated an engine change, but the aircraft was returned to service in time to take part in operations to relieve distress in Belize, devastated by 'Hurricane Hattie'. XL636 was retired to No. 5 MU on 22 December 1975 when defence cuts decimated RAF Transport Command, forcing the early retirement of the Belfast, Britannia and Comet and the disbandment of no fewer than seven squadrons. XL636 was then sold to Young Air Cargo and flown to Stansted on 6 May 1976 with the Belgian civil registration OO-YCE; it was delivered to Brussels on 13 May 1976 and was withdrawn from use again after a short working life with Youngs.

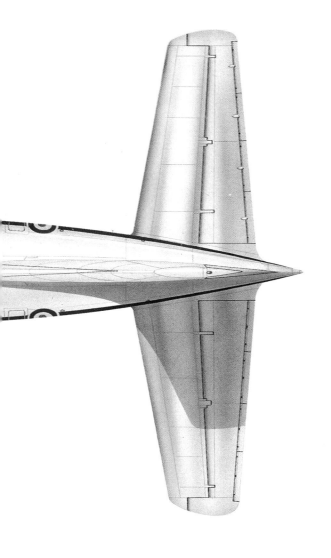

Specification
Bristol Type 175 Britannia Series 310
Type: long-range commercial transport
Powerplant: four 3072-ekW (4,120-eshp) Bristol 755 turboprops
Performance: maximum speed 639 km/h (397 mph); cruising speed 575 km/h (357 mph); service ceiling 7315 m (24,000 ft); range with maximum payload 6869 km (4,268 miles)
Weights: empty 37438 kg (82,537 lb); maximum take-off 83915 kg (185,000 lb)
Dimensions: span 43.36 m (142 ft 3 in); length 37.87 m (124 ft 3 in); height 11.43 m (37 ft 6 in); wing area 192.77 m² (2,075 sq ft)

Bristol Britannia variants

Bristol Type 175: original Bristol number for MRE aircraft, retained through all subsequent variants actually built in the UK
Britannia 101: two prototypes, G-ALBO with Mk 625 engines (later two Mk 705 and two Mk 755, then three Mk 755 and one Orion) and G-ALRX (four Mk 705)
Britannia 102: production for BOAC, short body, Mk 705 engines; total 15
Britannia 252: stretched long-range trooping aircraft built by Shorts (3) and used by RAF as **Britannia C.Mk 2**
Britannia 253: developed multi-role cargo aircraft built by Shorts, flown by RAF Nos 99 and 511 Sqns as **Britannia C.Mk 1**; total 20
Britannia 301: prototype of stretched civil version, G-ANCA
Britannia 302: two stretched aircraft without LR tanks, for Aeronaves de Mexico
Britannia 305: five similar to Series 302 but with LR tanks (but structure limited to 74843 kg/165,000 lb); built by Shorts for Northeast but sold to other customers
Britannia 312: 11 LR high-weight aircraft for BOAC, some later converted by other users to **Britannia 312F** for cargo
Britannia 313: three LR aircraft for El Al, later

joined by a fourth plus a Series 305 converted to **Britannia 306**
Britannia 314: six for Canadian Pacific, built by Shorts
Britannia 318: four for Cubana
Britannia 324: last two aircraft, built speculatively to latest standard, leased to CPA and then others
Bristol Type 189: unbuilt project for Nomad-engined MR version
Bristol Type 195: unbuilt project for high-wing military freighter (led to Short SC.5 Britannic, developed into Belfast)
Canadair CL-28: piston-engined MR aircraft produced for RCAF as **CP-107 Argus Mk 1** (13) and **Argus Mk 2** (20)
Canadair CL-44-6: stretched Tyne-engined version for RCAF as **CC-106 Yukon** (12)
Canadair CL-44D-4: improved civil swing-tail freighter built for Seaboard (seven **CL-44D-4-1**), Flying Tiger (12 **CL-44D-4-2**) and Slick (four **CL-44D-4-6**), and in passenger form for Loftleidir (three **CL-44D-4-8**)
Canadair CL-44J: further stretched passenger aircraft for Loftleidir (one plus three conversions)
Canadair CL-44O: single outsize rebuild by Conroy Aircraft from a CL-44D-4-2

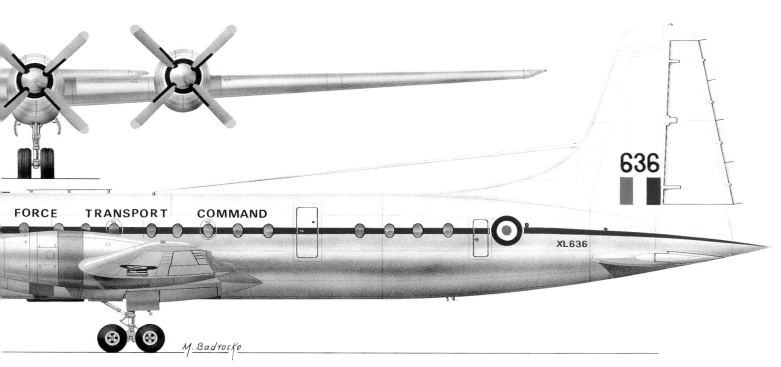

FORCE TRANSPORT COMMAND

636

XL636

M. Badrocke

BAC-111-500

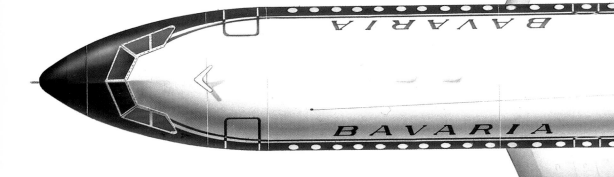

Entering service in 1965, the One-Eleven has outsold any other European airliner of recent times, and through a policy of consistent yet gradual improvement, the aircraft kept pace with other competitors until only recently. The original short-fuselage version was built in three variants, of which the Series 400 was the most popular, tailored for the North American market but also finding favour in other parts of the world. A fuselage stretch heralded the Series 500, which achieved splendid sales given the competition from Boeing and Douglas. This is a Series 414EG of Germanair/Bavaria Fluggesselschaft.

Specification
BAC-111-500
Wingspan: 28.5 m (93 ft 6 in)
Length: 32.61 m (107 ft 0 in)
Height: 7.47 m (24 ft 6 in)
Wing area: 95.78 m² (1,031 sq ft)
Powerplant: 2 × Rolls-Royce Spey 512DW, 12,550 lb thrust each
Passenger capacity: 119
Empty weight: 24454 kg (53,911 lb)
Maximum take-off weight: 47400 kg (104,500 lb)
Maximum cruising speed: 742 km/h (470 knots)
Service ceiling: 10670 m (35,000 ft)
Maximum range: 3484 km (1,880 nm)

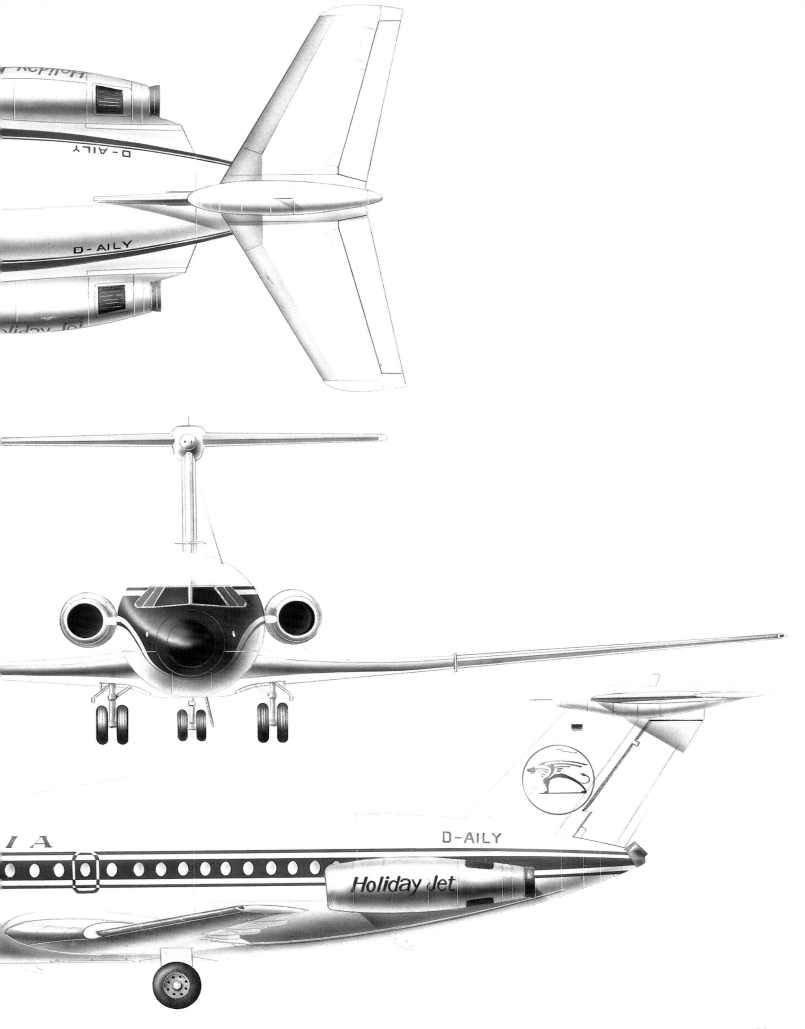

Handley-Page H.P.R.7 Dart Herald

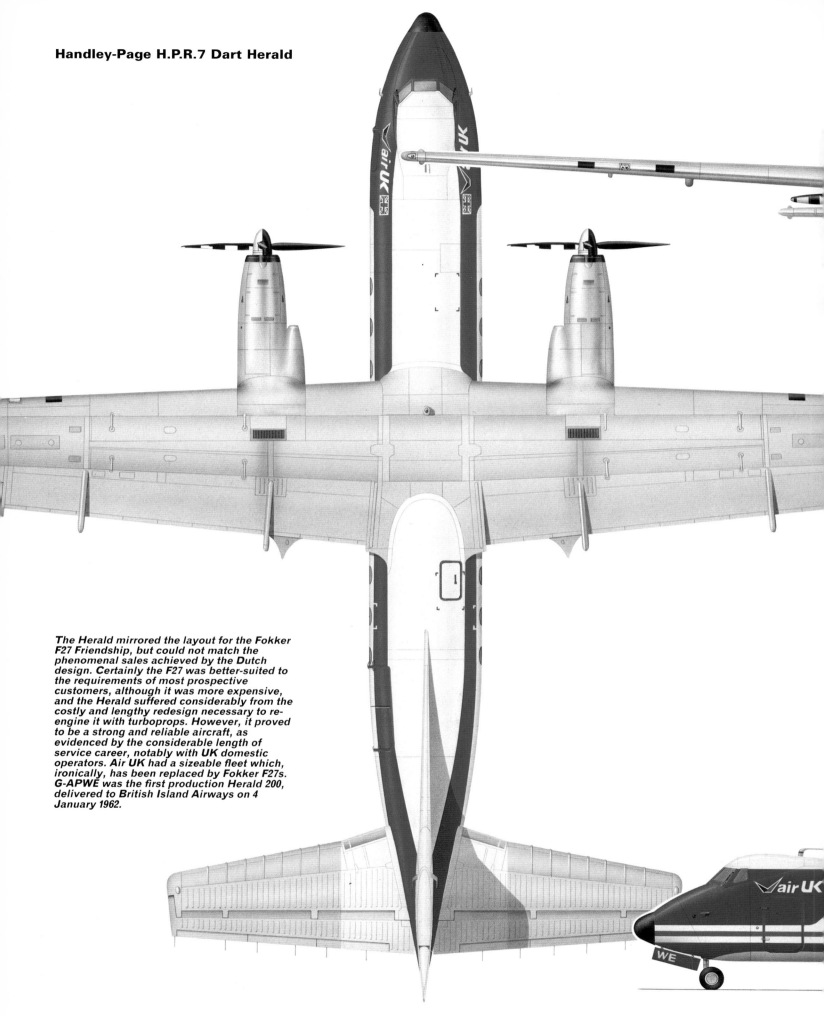

The Herald mirrored the layout for the Fokker F27 Friendship, but could not match the phenomenal sales achieved by the Dutch design. Certainly the F27 was better-suited to the requirements of most prospective customers, although it was more expensive, and the Herald suffered considerably from the costly and lengthy redesign necessary to re-engine it with turboprops. However, it proved to be a strong and reliable aircraft, as evidenced by the considerable length of service career, notably with UK domestic operators. Air UK had a sizeable fleet which, ironically, has been replaced by Fokker F27s. G-APWE was the first production Herald 200, delivered to British Island Airways on 4 January 1962.

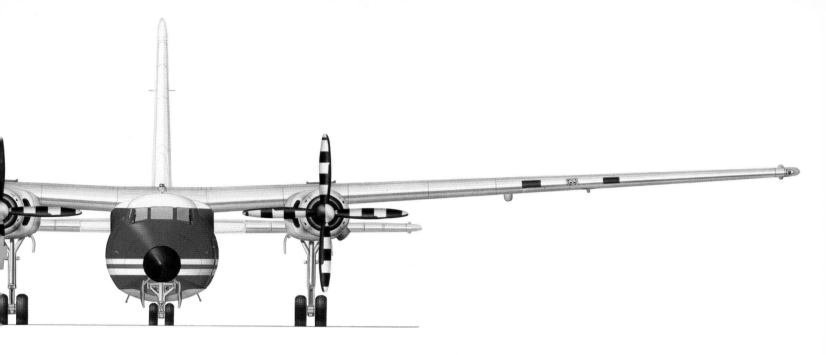

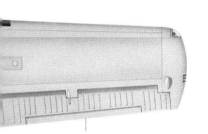

Specification
Handley-Page H.P.R.7 Dart Herald Series 200
Wingspan: 28.9 m (94 ft 9½ in)
Length: 23 m (75 ft 6 in)
Height: 7.34 m (24 ft 1 in)
Wing area: 82.3 m² (886 sq ft)
Powerplant: two 1570-kW (2,105-shp) Rolls-Royce Dart Mk 527 turboprops
Passenger capacity: 50-56
Empty weight: 11703 kg (25,800 lb)
Maximum take-off weight: 19505 kg (43,000 lb)
Maximum speed: 239 kt (170 km/h; 274 mph)
Cruising speed: 230 kt (164 km/h; 264 mph)
Service ceiling: 8504 m (27,900 ft)
Maximum range: 1,530 nm (2834 km; 1761 miles)
Range with maximum payload: 608 nm (1126 km; 700 miles)

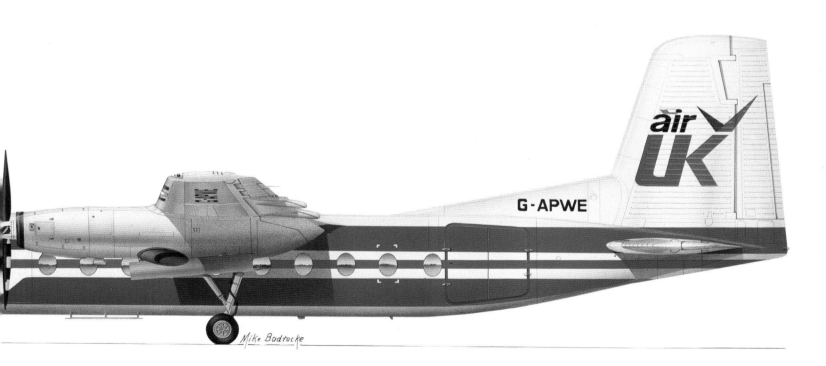

G-APWE

Mike Badrocke

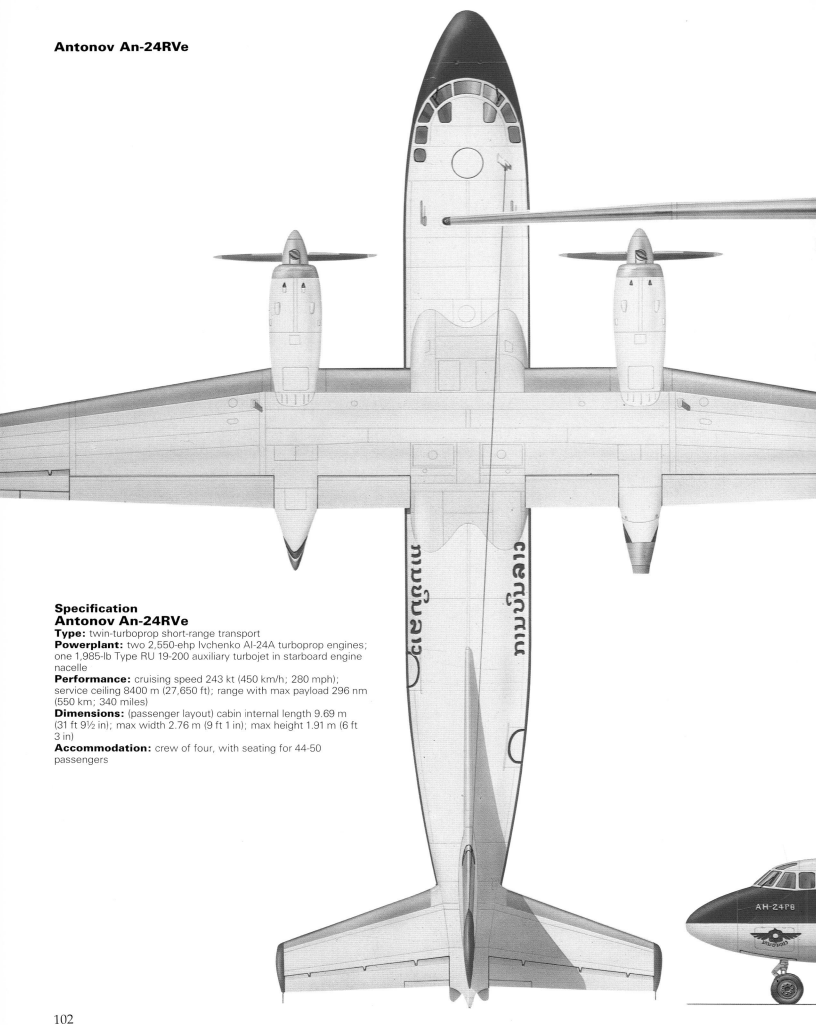

Antonov An-24RVe

Specification
Antonov An-24RVe

Type: twin-turboprop short-range transport

Powerplant: two 2,550-ehp Ivchenko AI-24A turboprop engines; one 1,985-lb Type RU 19-200 auxiliary turbojet in starboard engine nacelle

Performance: cruising speed 243 kt (450 km/h; 280 mph); service ceiling 8400 m (27,650 ft); range with max payload 296 nm (550 km; 340 miles)

Dimensions: (passenger layout) cabin internal length 9.69 m (31 ft 9½ in); max width 2.76 m (9 ft 1 in); max height 1.91 m (6 ft 3 in)

Accommodation: crew of four, with seating for 44-50 passengers

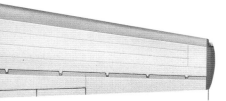

Based at the capital city of Lao, Laos'
national airline Lao Aviation is a pseudo-
military operator which operates a fleet of
three Antonov An-24RVs alongside a single
Chinese-built Xian Y-7-100. The An-24RV
carries an additional jet engine in the
starboard nacelle.

RDPL 3.4006

Mike Badrocke

**Antonov An-12BP
'Cub-A'**

GRANT RACE

104

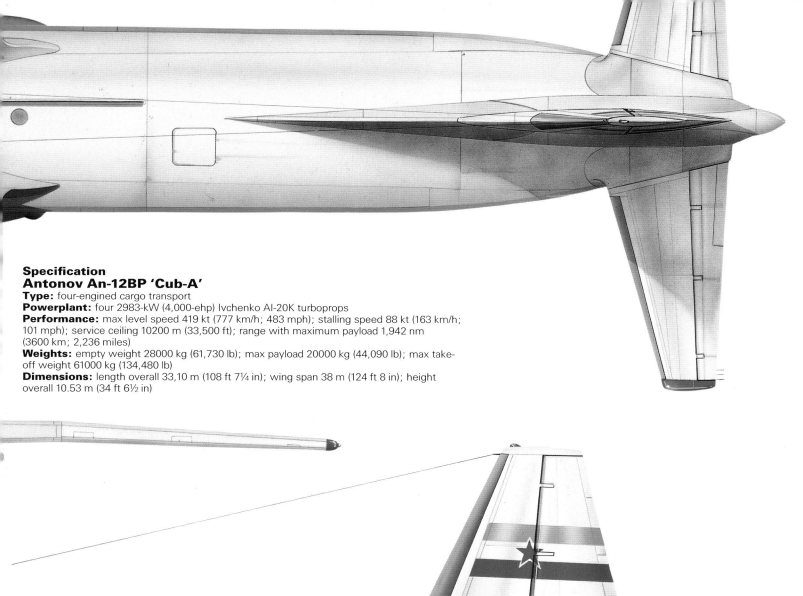

Specification
Antonov An-12BP 'Cub-A'
Type: four-engined cargo transport
Powerplant: four 2983-kW (4,000-ehp) Ivchenko AI-20K turboprops
Performance: max level speed 419 kt (777 km/h; 483 mph); stalling speed 88 kt (163 km/h; 101 mph); service ceiling 10200 m (33,500 ft); range with maximum payload 1,942 nm (3600 km; 2,236 miles)
Weights: empty weight 28000 kg (61,730 lb); max payload 20000 kg (44,090 lb); max take-off weight 61000 kg (134,480 lb)
Dimensions: length overall 33,10 m (108 ft 7¼ in); wing span 38 m (124 ft 8 in); height overall 10.53 m (34 ft 6½ in)

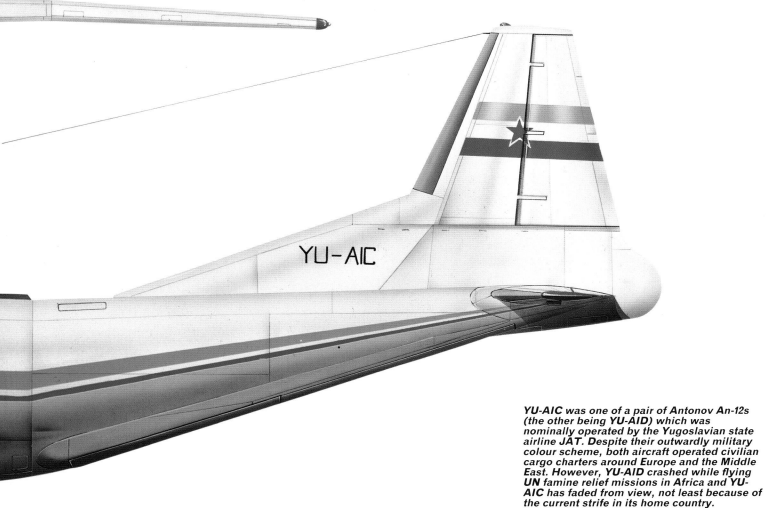

YU-AIC was one of a pair of Antonov An-12s (the other being YU-AID) which was nominally operated by the Yugoslavian state airline JAT. Despite their outwardly military colour scheme, both aircraft operated civilian cargo charters around Europe and the Middle East. However, YU-AID crashed while flying UN famine relief missions in Africa and YU-AIC has faded from view, not least because of the current strife in its home country.

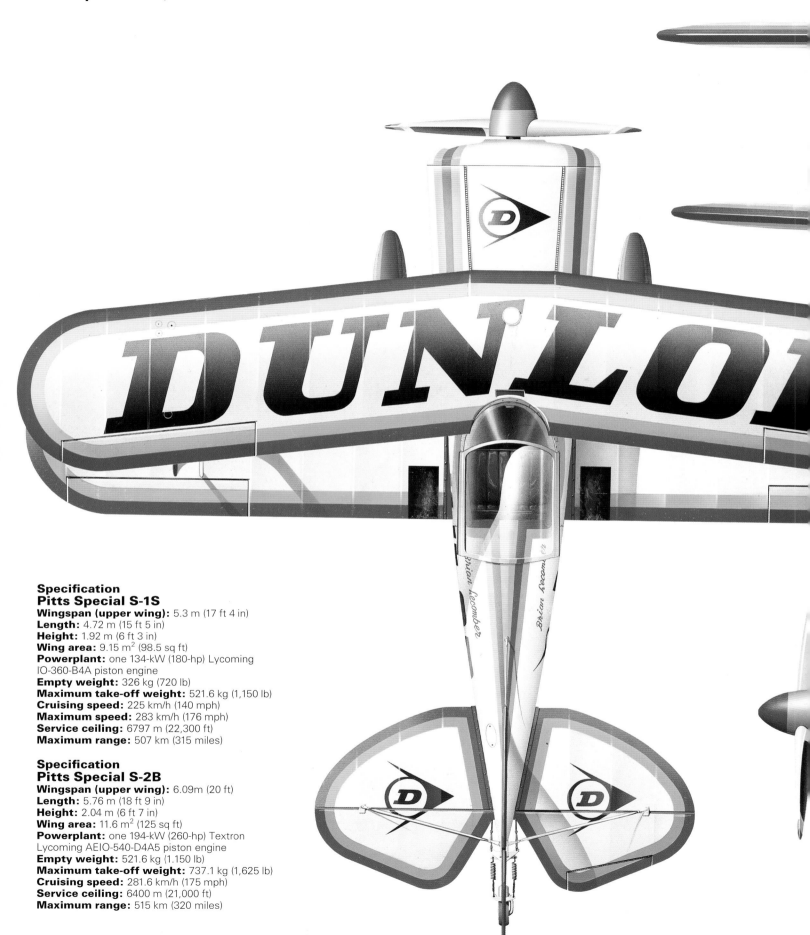

Specification
Pitts Special S-1S
Wingspan (upper wing): 5.3 m (17 ft 4 in)
Length: 4.72 m (15 ft 5 in)
Height: 1.92 m (6 ft 3 in)
Wing area: 9.15 m² (98.5 sq ft)
Powerplant: one 134-kW (180-hp) Lycoming
IO-360-B4A piston engine
Empty weight: 326 kg (720 lb)
Maximum take-off weight: 521.6 kg (1,150 lb)
Cruising speed: 225 km/h (140 mph)
Maximum speed: 283 km/h (176 mph)
Service ceiling: 6797 m (22,300 ft)
Maximum range: 507 km (315 miles)

Specification
Pitts Special S-2B
Wingspan (upper wing): 6.09m (20 ft)
Length: 5.76 m (18 ft 9 in)
Height: 2.04 m (6 ft 7 in)
Wing area: 11.6 m² (125 sq ft)
Powerplant: one 194-kW (260-hp) Textron
Lycoming AEIO-540-D4A5 piston engine
Empty weight: 521.6 kg (1.150 lb)
Maximum take-off weight: 737.1 kg (1,625 lb)
Cruising speed: 281.6 km/h (175 mph)
Service ceiling: 6400 m (21,000 ft)
Maximum range: 515 km (320 miles)

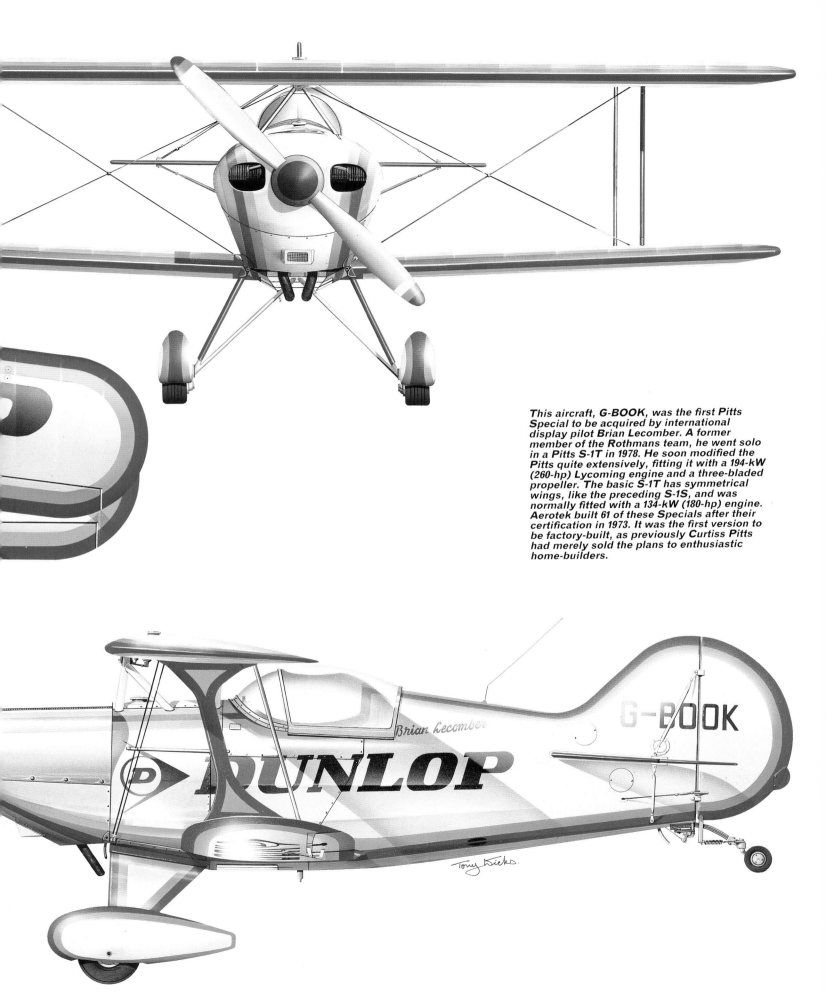

This aircraft, *G-BOOK*, was the first Pitts Special to be acquired by international display pilot Brian Lecomber. A former member of the Rothmans team, he went solo in a Pitts S-1T in 1978. He soon modified the Pitts quite extensively, fitting it with a 194-kW (260-hp) Lycoming engine and a three-bladed propeller. The basic S-1T has symmetrical wings, like the preceding S-1S, and was normally fitted with a 134-kW (180-hp) engine. Aerotek built 61 of these Specials after their certification in 1973. It was the first version to be factory-built, as previously Curtiss Pitts had merely sold the plans to enthusiastic home-builders.

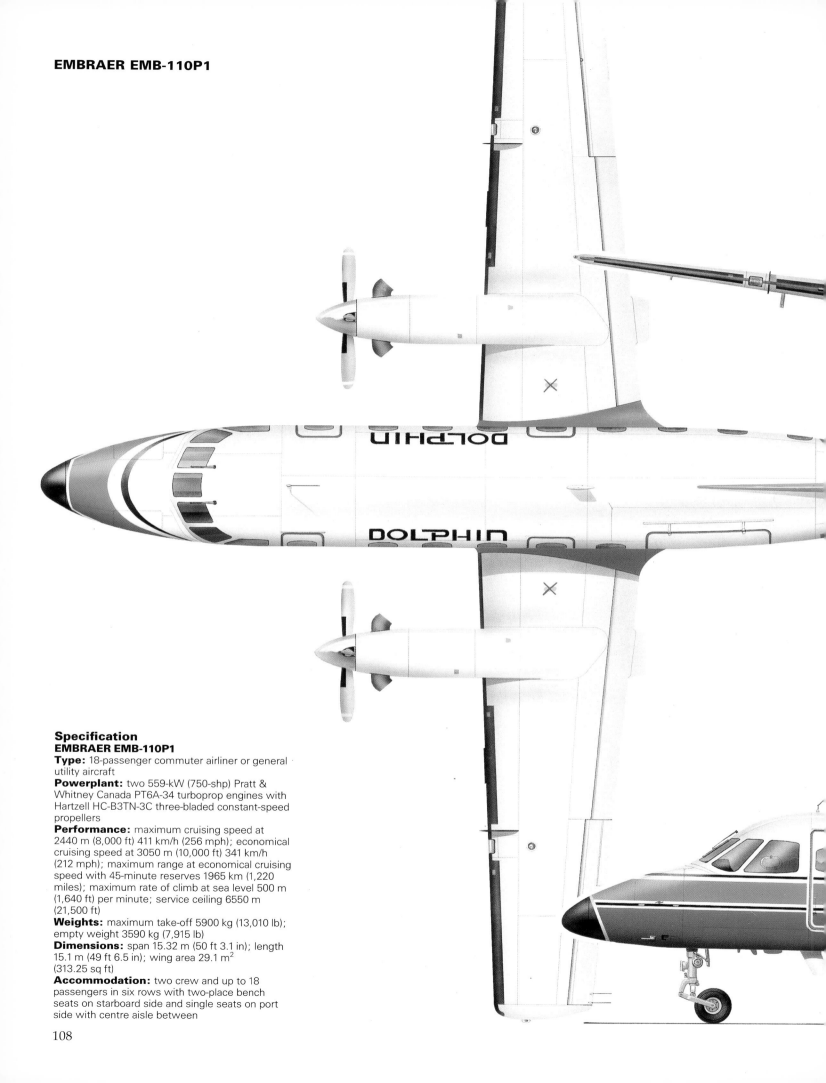

EMBRAER EMB-110P1

Specification
EMBRAER EMB-110P1

Type: 18-passenger commuter airliner or general utility aircraft

Powerplant: two 559-kW (750-shp) Pratt & Whitney Canada PT6A-34 turboprop engines with Hartzell HC-B3TN-3C three-bladed constant-speed propellers

Performance: maximum cruising speed at 2440 m (8,000 ft) 411 km/h (256 mph); economical cruising speed at 3050 m (10,000 ft) 341 km/h (212 mph); maximum range at economical cruising speed with 45-minute reserves 1965 km (1,220 miles); maximum rate of climb at sea level 500 m (1,640 ft) per minute; service ceiling 6550 m (21,500 ft)

Weights: maximum take-off 5900 kg (13,010 lb); empty weight 3590 kg (7,915 lb)

Dimensions: span 15.32 m (50 ft 3.1 in); length 15.1 m (49 ft 6.5 in); wing area 29.1 m^2 (313.25 sq ft)

Accommodation: two crew and up to 18 passengers in six rows with two-place bench seats on starboard side and single seats on port side with centre aisle between

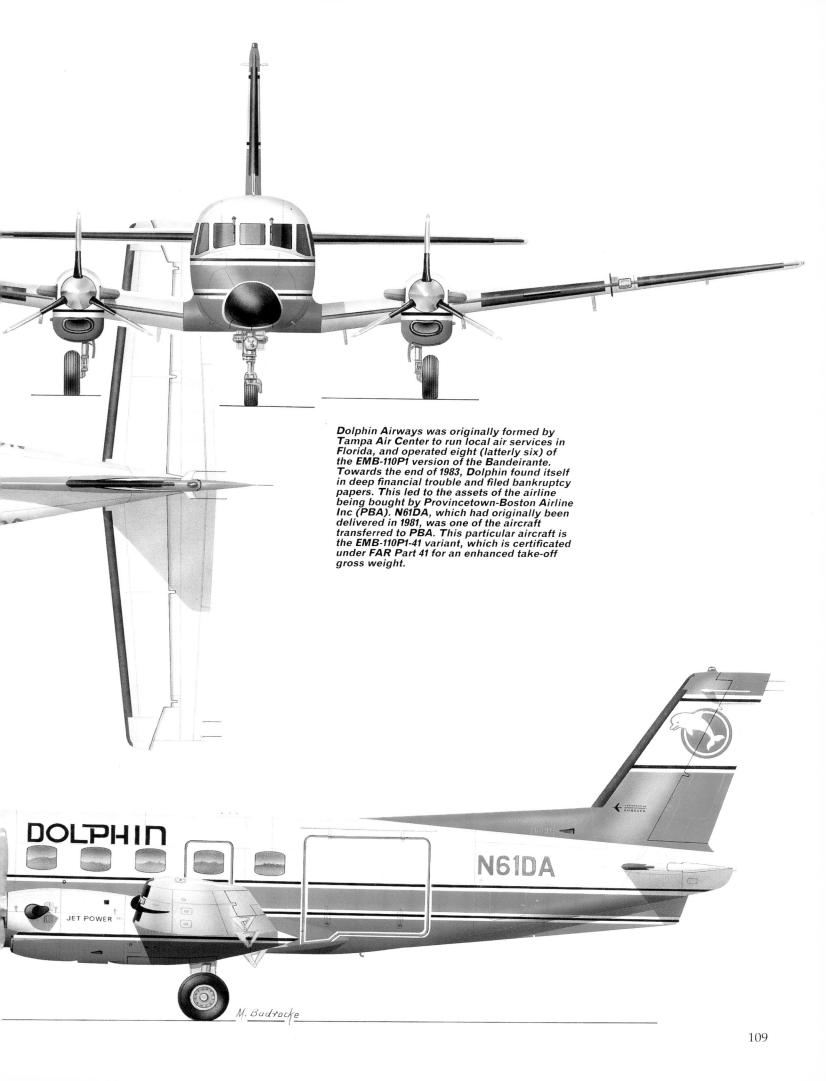

Dolphin Airways was originally formed by Tampa Air Center to run local air services in Florida, and operated eight (latterly six) of the EMB-110P1 version of the Bandeirante. Towards the end of 1983, Dolphin found itself in deep financial trouble and filed bankruptcy papers. This led to the assets of the airline being bought by Provincetown-Boston Airline Inc (PBA). N61DA, which had originally been delivered in 1981, was one of the aircraft transferred to PBA. This particular aircraft is the EMB-110P1-41 variant, which is certificated under FAR Part 41 for an enhanced take-off gross weight.

DOLPHIN

JET POWER

N61DA

M. Badrocke

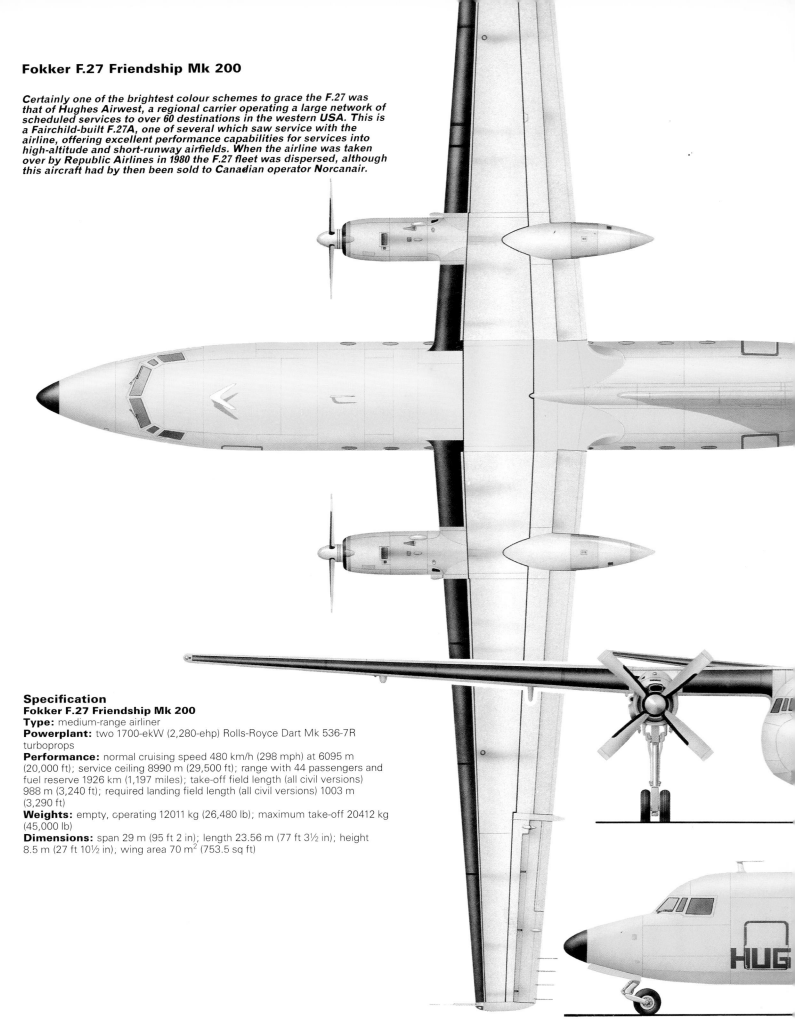

Fokker F.27 Friendship Mk 200

Certainly one of the brightest colour schemes to grace the F.27 was that of Hughes Airwest, a regional carrier operating a large network of scheduled services to over 60 destinations in the western USA. This is a Fairchild-built F.27A, one of several which saw service with the airline, offering excellent performance capabilities for services into high-altitude and short-runway airfields. When the airline was taken over by Republic Airlines in 1980 the F.27 fleet was dispersed, although this aircraft had by then been sold to Canadian operator Norcanair.

Specification
Fokker F.27 Friendship Mk 200
Type: medium-range airliner
Powerplant: two 1700-ekW (2,280-ehp) Rolls-Royce Dart Mk 536-7R turboprops
Performance: normal cruising speed 480 km/h (298 mph) at 6095 m (20,000 ft); service ceiling 8990 m (29,500 ft); range with 44 passengers and fuel reserve 1926 km (1,197 miles); take-off field length (all civil versions) 988 m (3,240 ft); required landing field length (all civil versions) 1003 m (3,290 ft)
Weights: empty, operating 12011 kg (26,480 lb); maximum take-off 20412 kg (45,000 lb)
Dimensions: span 29 m (95 ft 2 in); length 23.56 m (77 ft 3½ in); height 8.5 m (27 ft 10½ in), wing area 70 m² (753.5 sq ft)

Fokker F.27 variants

F.27-100: two prototypes (PH-NIV and NVF) as described in text
F.27-101 to 1118: standard production aircraft with Dart 511; total 85
F.27-200: standard basic aircraft with Dart 532, 536 or 551 engines; total 114
F.27-400 Combi: the Combiplane was the result of pressure from customers for a cargo or combined cargo/passenger version, with Dart 514 engines, a large cargo door, strong floor and quick-change passenger seats (typically stored overnight); total 13
F.27-300M Troopship: military variant of Mk 300, see Mk 400M
F.27-400 Combiplane: cargo or convertible version of Mk 200; total, with 400M, 171
F.27-400M: (name Troopship no longer used) military variant of standard aircraft with large cargo door, enlarged parachuting door on each side and fittings for 45 troop seats, 24 stretchers and nine seats or 5834 kg (12,862 lb) or (later aircraft) 6025 kg (13,283 lb) of cargo; sales include cartographic survey version with inertial navigation system and comprehensive camera and sight installations, and equipment for target towing
F.27-500: fuselage stretched 1.5 m (59 in), sold with and without cargo door; 15 aircraft for French PTT have large door both sides; total 97
F.27-500M: military variant of Mk 500
F.27-600: similar to Mk 200 but large cargo door only, with normal floor (but can be fitted with palletised seats and roller-track panels); total 47
F.27-700: Mk 600 offered with Dart 511 or 514; not built
F.27-800: redesignated 600RF
F.27-600RF: variant offered with rough-field landing gear (available on all models) with low-pressure tyres, long-stroke legs and greater ground clearance
F.27 Maritime: specialised maritime patrol variant for offshore patrol, SAR and all other maritime duties with tankage for 12-hour endurance with crew of (typically) six, with numerous detail changes throughout aircraft, including clearance to 21320 kg (47,003 lb), equipment including Litton APS-504 search radar, Bendix weather radar and extremely comprehensive nav/com systems, as well as bubble observation windows, tactical compartment and crew rest area; total 14
F.27 Maritime Enforcer: armed version of Maritime with provision for anti-shipping missiles or other weapons on wing pylons, and special equipment
F-27: basic Fairchild (later Fairchild-Hiller) 16193-kg (35,700-lb) version with Dart 511 or 511-7E with water/methanol hot-day power restoration as available on all F.27s
F-27A: uprated Dart 528 or 528-7E version cleared to 19050 kg (42,000 lb) and equivalent to Mk 200
F-27B: large cargo door and cargo or convertible interior, originally cleared only to 17463 kg (38,500 lb)
F-27F: executive version with uprated Mk 529-7E engines and optional long-range tanks
F-27G: proposed F-27F for airlines; not built
F-27J: final standard pre-stretch model with Dart 532-7 engines
F-27M: hot/high version with Dart 532-7 engines driving 3.66-m (12-ft) propellers; final US-built variant
FH-227: Fairchild-developed version with fuselage stretch of 1.83 m (6 ft), Mk 532-7 engines, cleared to 19731 kg (43,500 lb)
FH-227B: developed long-fuselage version with redesigned windscreens, strengthened landing gears, thicker wing skins and reinforced rear fuselage, Dart 532-7s driving 3.81-m (12-ft 6-in) propellers; maximum weight 20638 kg (45,500 lb)
FH-227C: FH-227 modified by field kit with FH-227B changes but still held to 19731 kg (43,500 lb)
FH-227D: final new-build stretched model with Mk 532-7L engines, intermediate take-off flap setting and anti-skid brakes
FH-227E: FH-227 modified by field kit with Mk 532-7L engines and other FH-227D improvements but with unchanged structure
Cargonaut: modification by California Airmotive with forward freight door and internal provisions for palletised cargo
Fokker 50: new-generation development with PW124 engines and updated airframe and systems

M. Badrocke
'84